THE BIG STEP

The Big Step

How to Survive Islam in the Anglosphere

And Thrive Outside of It

(And avoid convert abuse)

Copyright ©Mahdi Lock

The moral right of Mahdi Lock to be identified as the author of this
work has been asserted.

This is a work of non-fiction.

All rights reserved, including the right to reproduce this book or portions
thereof in any form whatsoever. Any person who does any unauthorised act in
relation to this publication may be liable to criminal prosecution and civil
claims for damages.

To contact the author or for further information regarding special discounts
for bulk purchases, please send an email to nwmlock@gmail.com.

Distributed by www.lulu.com

Published by The Foreword Publications

Cover design by Kashif Ahmed: kashif_ahmad1984@yahoo.co.uk

ISBN 978-0-244-03301-9

4

Table of Contents

Chapter 1: Why become Muslim?

"So where are you going?" [at-Takwīr 81:26]

Today is the 15th anniversary of the 9/11 attacks. If there is one seminal event that has defined and shaped Islam in the Anglosphere, what happened that Tuesday morning in 2001 is it. It was also a fork in the road. How would Muslims in the Anglosphere, particularly in the United States, respond? Would they demonstrate that this is what a dangerous and heretical theology leads to, which is the direction that they had been heading in, or would they perform an about turn and embrace ecumenism?

The answer, if you have not noticed, is the latter, and whatever hope there was for Islam in the Anglosphere has been drowned and depleted. Terrorist attacks continue to happen and the theology that the overwhelming majority of terrorists cling to, as well as those who sympathise with them, continues to spread its tentacles in the English-speaking world.

What does any of the above have to do with the choice to become Muslim? Islam is not a social club, and it is more than just a religion. It is not a good idea to join because you need friends, or you have just had some crisis in your life, like a divorce or a lost job, or you need some discipline in your life due to alcoholism or drug abuse. Being a Muslim may help in these situations, but they should not be *the* reason and motive that makes you decide to be a Muslim.

It is not a good idea to become Muslim because you think it is cool and trendy and part of the counter-culture or an expression of rebellion against the establishment. It is also not a good idea to become Muslim because you find Islam to be quaint and interesting, or you like the food and the traditional dress. Islam is not a fetish. It is not a vehicle for you to live out your fantasies of dressing up like Lawrence of Arabia, or some spiritual master from a bygone era. Whether you look like Batman or Bruce Wayne, becoming a Muslim means that you become you. You realise and recognise who you are in the grand scheme of things, who you belong to and what your responsibilities are.

This is why 9/11 is important. It was a wake-up call and a reminder of what I've said above. It was a reminder that, very quickly, it can become incredibly uncool to be Muslim. Those interesting clothes quickly come to be seen as threatening and intimidating. Thinking that Islam is so "spiritual" no longer appeals when the religion is associated with death and destruction.

So why should you become a Muslim? The answer is simple: conviction. You have to be convinced that it is the absolute truth. You have to realise that it will not make you popular. People who loved you will stop loving you. People whom you hoped would love you never will. Some people will go as far as actually hating you, maybe some will want to cause you harm. Salvation is a free gift from Allah, but it could cost you your life.

To become a Muslim means to declare oneself unreconciled to the world. This is not your only abode or your permanent abode.

It is a seedbed for the Hereafter, nothing more and nothing less. Imam ʿAlī ibn Abī Ṭālib, may Allah be pleased with him, is reported to have said, 'Prepare for this life as if you are going to live forever. Prepare for the next life as if you are going to die tomorrow.' Think about what your life would be like if the inverse of that advice were followed. You wouldn't develop yourself, educate yourself or hold any ambitions or goals because you could die tomorrow, but you wouldn't pray or fast or do anything to draw nearer to your Lord because you could have a long life, and time is on your side.

The great Egyptian scholar, Imam Muḥammad Mutawallī ash-Shaʿrawī, may Allah have mercy on him, was asked about the apostasy ruling in Islam, i.e. why is it written in our law books that an apostate can be executed? His answer was that this ruling has more to do with people entering the faith than people leaving it. The wisdom is quality control. People who enter the fold should be high-quality and low-maintenance, not low-quality and high-maintenance. The apostasy ruling is there to deter freeloaders, sob storytellers, hypocrites, charlatans, hippie savants, and so forth.

The ruling also informs as to how we Muslims are to present the faith and call to it. We have to be forthright and honest, which is part of what this book aims to do. We cannot water down our beliefs and laws in the hope that we can offer a form of Islam that is acceptable to the person being preached to. This is a lost cause. Even if this person does state the testimony of faith, there are two major problems. For starters, if this person had to be lied to in order to be convinced of the faith, it means he or she will be high-maintenance. Secondly, it will only be a matter of time before this person discovers more about Islam on their own, realises that it is not actually what they signed up for and then they will leave. Convert recidivism is real, very real.

Islam is for everyone and it is not for everyone. It is offered to everyone but not everyone is going to accept it. The Lord made this clear in the Qur'an, in Surat al-'Arāf (7:172) when He had all of humanity testify that He is indeed their Lord. They testified in the affirmative, all of them, but, as Imam Ibn al-Jawzī points out in his commentary, not every single person was honest. In fact, the majority lied. Whatever decision was made at that point in history is the decision that affects the life of every single human on this earth, in every time and place. If you testified that Allah is your Lord and you meant it, you will be saved. If you did not, you will not. The pen has been lifted and the ink has dried.

Does that mean that preaching the faith is pointless? No. We do not know who those people are. We do not know who meant it and who did not. There are people who are ostensibly disbelievers right now, but they meant it, and there are those who are ostensibly Muslim now and they did not mean it. In the fourth ḥadīth of his famous collection of forty, Imam an-Nawawī, may Allah be pleased with him, quotes the Messenger of Allah, may Allah bless him and grant him peace, explaining that someone will do the actions of the people of Paradise until there is only a cubit between him and it, and then what has been written will catch up with him and he will become from the people of the Fire and enter it. Likewise, there will be those who

10

do the actions of the people of the Fire until there is only a cubit between them and the Fire, and then what has been written will catch up with them and they will become from the people of Paradise and enter it.

Therefore, we have to present the faith; that is not questioned. Secondly, we have to present the faith honestly and truthfully, with good manners of course, but honestly and truthfully. That is what the Lord has commanded us to do, in several verses in His Book. For example, in Sūrat Yā Sīn, the 36th chapter in the 17th verse, Allah says, **"And there is nothing upon us except the clear conveyance of the message."** Yes, there is also reward if someone is guided to Islam through you, but we want quality, not quantity. How can there be reward if that same person leaves Islam a few weeks, months or even years later? We want potential converts to fully grasp and understand what they are committing themselves to. Once that has been achieved, and we can be reassured that they will not feel deceived and tricked later on down the line, then we happily accept their testimony of faith and whatever happens after that we leave to Allah. The foolishness of rushing people to articulate the testimony of faith will be discussed in the next chapter.

When one's main motive for becoming a Muslim is conviction, conviction will be the main motive for every decision made thereafter. Are you going to be an Orthodox (i.e. Sunnī) Muslim or are you going to join one of the cults? If you choose the former, you will then choose one of the four legal schools based on what you think is best for you. You won't change it depending on where you are or who you're with, because you want to fit in and feel comfortable. Fitting in and feeling comfortable was not your motive for becoming Muslim in the first place. The presence of conviction, or the lack thereof, will also be visible in what spiritual path you join (aka Sufi ṭarīqah), or if you join one at all.

To further understand this phenomenon, and especially in the Anglosphere, I would highly recommend the book *The True Believer: Thoughts on the Nature of Mass Movements* by Eric Hoffer. The main thesis is that people join movements (religions, political parties, political activist organisations, spiritual brotherhoods etc.) because they fear an autonomous existence. In other words, these people are scared or do not have the confidence to live their lives on their own terms and to tell themselves what to do. They would much prefer to delegate that authority, or indeed responsibility, to someone else.

Therefore, as Hoffer stresses, these people couldn't care less about the doctrines of the movement or group they belong to. What matters to them is that they *belong* to something. This also explain why you will see these people moving from group to group easily and even frequently, despite the doctrines being radically different. For example, someone might start in a political group with heretical Mu'tazilite theology, and spend a great deal of their time talking about how the Muslim laity must restore the Caliphate. Some time later, that same individual will have joined a Sufi tariqa, and will be spending most of his time talking about how "spiritual" he feels and how amazing it is to go into a state of spiritual ecstasy every Thursday. A few years later, it would not be implausible to find that person amongst the ranks of Greenpeace. In 2011, I wrote a review of this book entitled 'Madness is Rare In Individuals', which includes the following:

'The second matter is the desire for substitutes. Hoffer explains that the difference between a mass movement and a practical organisation is that the latter offers opportunities for self-advancement while the former satisfies the passion for self-renunciation. This a is constant theme throughout the book, which is that mass movements appeal to the fear of an autonomous existence, an existence in which one has to think for oneself, and of course, this dovetails nicely with the objectives of compulsory schools.'[1]

But where does this fear of an autonomous existence come from? Why do such people lack the confidence and willpower to tell themselves what to do? Why do they feel the need to refer and defer to "experts"? As this is a book about the Anglosphere, it would be wise to look at the educational system that is present in these countries, and the best and most concise description of what happens in the schools is found in John Taylor Gatto's book *Dumbing Us Down*. Gatto focuses less on the subject material that is taught in schools and more on the structures and methods that are employed, such as students being classified into age groups, classes starting and ending with bells, students being made to rely on their teachers for emotional and intellectual validation, and so forth. Several years ago, I wrote in my review of Gatto's book (entitled 'Western Mass Education'),

---

[1] http://mahdinnm.blogspot.com/2013/11/madness-is-rare-in-individuals.html (Accessed July 12, 2018)

'The fourth and fifth lessons are **emotional dependency** and **intellectual dependency**. The first is a direct attack against individuality. Pupils are not allowed to express any form of individuality but instead must conform to the system. As for the latter, intellectual dependency, Gatto says: "This is the most important lesson of them all: we must wait for other people, better trained than ourselves, to make the meanings of our lives." Is it any wonder that so many of these brainwashing organisations exist and are flourishing in the west, from Greenpeace to Salafiyyah to a whole host of 'sufi' tareeqas? As Gatto says, "Good people wait for an expert to tell them what to do. It is hardly an exaggeration to say that our entire economy depends on this lesson being learned. Think of what might fall apart if children weren't trained to be dependent: the social services could hardly survive – they would vanish, I think, into the recent historical limbo out of which they arose. Counsellors and therapists would look on in horror as the supply of psychic invalids vanished. Commercial entertainment of all sorts, including television, would wither as people learned again how to make their own fun. Restaurants, the prepared food industry, and a whole host of other assorted food services would be drastically down-sized if people returned to making their own meals rather than depending on strangers to plant, pick, chop, and cook for them. Much of modern law, medicine, and engineering would go too, as well as the clothing business and school teaching, unless a guaranteed supply of helpless people continued to pour out of our schools each year…We've built a way of life that depends on people doing what they are told because they don't know how to tell *themselves* what to do."[2]

---

[2] http://mahdinnm.blogspot.com/2013/11/madness-is-rare-in-individuals.html (Accessed July 12, 2018)

So, in the Anglosphere and much of Europe, children are raised to fear an autonomous existence, and this makes them easy prey, when talking about Muslim children, for the various organisations and cults that have free reign in such lands. I say 'free reign' because many of these groups have no hope of gaining any traction in the traditional Muslim heartlands. Their peoples by and large reject them and their governments clamp down on them. This phenomenon will be discussed later in this book when talking about the growing divide between Islam itself and Anglosphere Islam.

Self-renunciation vs. self-advancement is also a good measure for looking at the difference between Muslim Orthodoxy, or the majority of Muslims, and the organisations and cults that flourish in the Anglosphere. As I mentioned before, becoming Muslim is about becoming you, about becoming who you truly are, a slave of Allah, and recognising and acknowledging where you belong in the grand scheme of things. This is self-advancement, or the betterment of oneself. Self-renunciation is quite the opposite. I have seen converts to Islam adopt a fanatical, almost monastic, attitude to life after embracing Islam. They no longer care about their personal hygiene, their appearance, professional qualifications, education, career advancement and so on and so forth. All of these things are deemed "worldly", but Allah Himself has said, **"Monasticism, they invented it. We did not prescribe it for them."** [al-Ḥadīd 57: 37] Having worldly possessions or a worldly status, i.e. having the world in your hand, is not the same as having the world in your heart. As long as your heart loves Allah and you understand that these possessions and status will either leave you (i.e. you will lose them in this life) or you will leave them when you die, there is nothing blameworthy therein. There are wealthy Prophets, such as Dāwūd and Sulaymān, peace be upon them, and there are wealthy Companions, such as Abū Bakr, ʿUthmān, ʿAbdur Raḥmān ibn ʿAwf, az-Zubayr and Ṭalḥah, may Allah be pleased with all of them.[3] Earning a living, and even being good at it, does not contradict relying on Allah. Imam Muḥammad ibn al-Ḥasan al-Shaybānī says in his *Kitāb al-Kasb*:

'This fact was clarified by ʿUmar, may Allāh be pleased with him, in his ḥadīth (in which it is reported) that he came by a group of people from among the devoted worshippers and saw them sitting, drooping their heads, and so he said, "Who are those?," and it was said (to him), "Those are the reliant (i.e. on Allāh)", whereupon he said, "Definitely not! But rather they are the devourers, who devour the wealth of people! Shall I not tell you who the reliant are?" and it was said to him, "Yes." He said, "The reliant is he who casts a seed into the soil and then places his reliance on his Lord, Most Exalted, Most Glorious." In another narration about him, he said, "O assembly of devoted worshippers, raise your heads and earn (a living) for your souls."'[4]

---

[3] Please see this ruling by Imam ʿAbdul Ḥalīm Maḥmood:
http://mahdinnm.blogspot.com/2018/01/can-muslim-be-communist.html
(Accessed July 12, 2018)
[4] Translated into English by Adi Setia as *The Book of Earning a Livelihood* (Kuala Lumpur: IBFIM, 2011), p.20-21

16

Therefore, to summarise what has been stated, we can say that the ship of salvation welcomes anyone and everyone on board, but once you're on board, it's all hands on deck. Allah makes this clear when He says, **"They think they have done you a favour by becoming Muslims! Say, 'Do not consider your Islam a favour to me. No indeed! It is Allah who has favoured you by guiding you to faith if you are telling the truth.'"** [al-Ḥujurāt 49:17] One thus enters Islam with conviction and with that conviction one seeks to serve Allah and His religion, not to be served.

Chapter 2: The Testimony of Faith...and then what?

"The desert Arabs say, 'We believe!' Say: 'You do not believe. Say rather, "We have become Muslim", for faith has not yet entered into your hearts.'" [al-Ḥujurāt 49:14]

A very disturbing phenomenon of Anglosphere Islam is what I call "the Shahādah scorecards", i.e. this competition amongst "preachers" (I use that term loosely) to get as many people as possible to state the testimony of faith: 'I bear witness that there is no god but Allah and I bear witness that Muḥammad is the Messenger of Allah.'

As mentioned before, there is reward in someone being guided to Islam through you. The Messenger of Allah, may Allah bless him and grant him peace, said, {For Allah to guide one person through you is better than red camels.} As Imam an-Nawawī, may Allah have mercy on him, explains in his commentary of the ḥadīth, red camels signify something immensely precious. He also goes on to say that this ḥadīth elucidates the virtue of knowledge, calling to guidance and establishing good practices.[5]

Take a minute to think about what Imam an-Nawawī has stated. This ḥadīth elucidates the virtue of knowledge and calling to guidance. As for guidance itself, this is for Allah to do. He, the Exalted, says in His Book, **"When Allah desires to guide**

---

[5] *Ṣaḥīḥ Muslim bi Sharḥ an-Nawawī* (Beirut: Dār al-Kutub al-ʿIlmiyyah, 1423/2003), v.15, p.144-145

someone, He opens His heart to Islam." [al-Anʿām 6:125] Our job is to present the faith, not to make people accept it.

Nonetheless, those looking to get the highest "shahādah score" and some convert trophies to put on display use the abovementioned ḥadīth as proof for what they're doing. They will boast about the hundreds and even thousands of people that have "taken the shahādah" at their hands.[6] But is stating the testimony of faith the same as being guided?

A *New Statesman* article, dated May 17, 2013, starts with the words, 'Over 100,000 people in Britain converted to Islam between 2001 and 2011, yet it is believed that up to 75 per cent may have since lost their faith.'[7] Obviously, there is a lack of quality control. Who is stating the testimony of faith and outwardly becoming Muslims? What are their motives? What were they looking for? It certainly doesn't look like conviction played a part.

Amongst the reasons for leaving mentioned in the article, one is abuse. Pepe, for example, left the faith because he was being abused by a cult-like ṣūfī ṭarīqah that tried to control more and more of his life. Other people left because of the narrow-mindedness of Muslims. Reasons like this are not very hard to believe. Pimping the religion, as in the first case, and woeful ignorance are dominant facets of Anglosphere Islam.

---

[6] See this as an example: http://hasbunallah.com.au/khalidyasin/ (Accessed Sept 29, 2016)

[7] http://www.newstatesman.com/religion/2013/05/confessions-ex-muslim (Accessed Sept 29, 2016)

As discussed in an article[8] by Al-Hajj Abu Ja'far al-Hanbali, converts are not being vetted. If someone has an interest in Islam, the typical response you will find in the Anglosphere is to pounce. 'He must take the shahādah as soon as possible! What if he dies tonight?' So Allah's decree is not final? What was said and what was meant when Allah made all of humanity testify before Him can be altered and changed *now*? Are there Muslim storybooks somewhere entitled *The Muslim that Slipped Through the Net* or *The Non-Muslim That Got Away*?

The answer is no, because Allah's decree is final. We don't have to rush anyone into becoming Muslim. Our job is to present the faith. It all goes back to the testimony that was given when humanity was asked, 'Am I not your Lord?'[9] Those who affirmed it and meant it will die as Muslims and attain salvation. Those who affirmed it and did not mean it will not attain salvation. Convert recidivism should be clear proof, in addition to what we find in the Revelation, that saying the testimony of faith does not mean that someone is ultimately saved.

This should drastically change our approach to preaching. Instead of rushing and panicking, if someone shows interest in Islam, we should sit them down and patiently explain things to them, even if it takes months or years. If they are meant to be saved they will be saved. What we want and seek is a high-quality, low-maintenance convert, and if they don't become Muslim, their

---

[8] Please see https://jurjis.wordpress.com/2013/06/06/it-was-no-surprise/ (Accessed Sept 29, 2016)
[9] Please see Sūrat al-ʾAʿrāf 7:172

matter rests with Allah. If they are to be Muslim, it may be that we are not the means through which this will come to pass. Either way, we've done our job, which is to present and convey the faith.

What we have instead, in the Anglosphere, is "preachers" pressuring people and rushing them to state the testimony of faith, and then problems tarise from both parties. The "preachers" do not engage in any vetting: does this potential convert have any psychological issues? Does he or she have any drug or alcohol problems? Does he or she fully understand what they are getting into? Could they be using Islam as a vehicle or outlet for something else? The one being preached to has to ask: do I understand what I am getting into? Am I convinced of Islam or is Islam merely meeting a need that I have at this point in time? If my needs changed, would I still be Muslim?

As demonstrated in the article referenced above, the result is high-maintenance, low-quality converts, many of whom use Islam as a vehicle for their resentment and bitterness towards their society and the world in general.[10] These converts then become easy prey for the cornucopia of groups and cults that run wild in the Anglosphere.[11] Those who fall into the snares of the politicised, radical elements can end up being involved in

---

[10] On that note, I highly recommend this article on ginger British converts: http://www.breitbart.com/london/2014/09/09/ginger-jihadis-why-redheads-are-attracted-to-radical-islam/ (Accessed Sept 29, 2016) Gingers, especially in the UK, are mercilessly mocked and bullied in childhood.

[11] Please see this article from *The New York Times*: http://www.nytimes.com/2006/08/17/world/europe/17converts.html?_r=0 (Accessed Sept 29, 2016)

terrorism, from planning through to perpetrating, and when they are caught, those same "preachers" and the people at the masjids they used to frequent claim to have no knowledge of them. In the press, we will read statements like, "He only prayed here a few times." "He was quiet, didn't really speak to people." "We had no idea he was capable of such a thing." And so forth.

These are the horrific consequences of keeping shahādah scorecards and treating converts (potential and actual) like trophies. This is convert abuse.

And to understand the motives that push these groups in the Anglosphere (who are mainly there because they can't get a foothold in the Muslim world) to pounce on converts and use them to swell their ranks, I think Eric Hoffer, in *The True Believer*, has the best explanation:

'Intensity of conviction is not the main factor which impels a movement to spread its faith to the four corners of the earth: "religions of great intensity often confine themselves to contemning, destroying, or at best pitying what is not themselves."[12] Nor is the impulse to proselytize an expression of an overabundance of power which as Bacon has it "is like a great flood, that will be sure to overflow."[13] The missionary zeal seems rather an expression of some deep misgiving, some pressing feeling of insufficiency at the centre. Proselytizing is more a passionate search for something not yet found than a desire to bestow upon the world something we already have. It is a search for a final and

---

[12] Jacob Burckhardt, *Force and Freedom* (New York: Pantheon Books, 1943), p.129

[13] Francis Bacon, "Of Vicissitude of Things," Bacon's *Essays*, Everyman's Library Edition (New York: E.P. Dutton and Company, 1932) p.171

irrefutable demonstration that our absolute truth is indeed the one and only truth. The proselytizing fanatic strengthens his own faith by converting others. The creed whose legitimacy is most easily challenged is likely to develop the strongest proselytizing impulse.'[14]

And thus, we have one of the major ways in which converts are abused in the Anglosphere. They are simply tokens of validation for the adherents of these groups and Muslim Brotherhood front organisations. This will be discussed further in the next chapter.

---

[14] p.110

Chapter 3: Who actually cares about you?

"Do people imagine that they will be left to say, 'We believe' and will not be tested?" [al-ʿAnkabūt 29:2]

How do you avoid being a token of validation for someone else? How do you find people that will genuinely and sincerely help you instead of offering to help while actually seeking to use you for some nefarious end?

When becoming a Muslim, there are two basic areas of need: social and educational. You will need other Muslims around, people you can talk to, eat with and pray with. Islam is a community-based religion, and this should be obvious from looking at the central role that the masjid plays in Muslim life. As for the educational side, you will need to learn who your Lord is, which is covered in theology, and how to worship Him, which is covered in law, or *fiqh*.

In the Muslim world, and especially in the olden days, a convert can be integrated very quickly. He can state the testimony of faith at a masjid, and thereby meet the congregation that pray there, and then attend the classes that take place at the masjid, in theology, fiqh, Arabic and so forth. It was also a standard practice that a convert would be assigned a guide, or *murshid*, who would advise him through the early stages until he was ready to progress and develop on his own.

In the Anglosphere, there is something called "New Muslim" projects, or organisations, and I've worked directly with them in the United Kingdom. I certainly do not want to knock the efforts of the believing brothers and sisters who work hard and put a lot of time and effort into these projects, and almost entirely voluntarily, but the very fact that these organisations exist presents a question: what are the masjids doing? Why are converts being looked after by organisations that are separate from the local masjid?

The sad and obvious answer is that the vast majority of masjids are not catering to the needs of converts. Even in the Anglosphere, converts will struggle to find a Friday *khutbah* in English, let alone classes. There will be *khutbahs* in Arabic, and this is understandable as Arabic is the language of Islam, but a lot of the lecturing and teaching will be in the languages of people that migrated to the Anglosphere, and this is especially the case with South Asians in the United Kingdom and their insistence on their native language.[15] In fact, many of them regard English as "the language of the enemy" and therefore it is somehow insulting to Islam to use it for any religious function, such as teaching and preaching. I was told this by a Pakistani imam who had the gumption to start giving sermons in English, and long before any other imam did.

At this point, I could go off on a tangent and ask why Pakistanis, for example, would come to England in the first place if English is "the language of the enemy". Why do some of them, such as the owner of the London School of Islamics, insist on Urdu being

---

[15] This is especially the case with Pakistanis, who tend to regard Urdu as "an Islamic language" on par with Arabic

taught in British schools[16] and decry that Pakistani children being taught English in the same schools is a form of "cultural imperialism"?

Nevertheless, this attitude hampers the integration of converts into the Muslim community, or indeed begs the question: is there a Muslim community or do we have several communities (Pakistani, Bangladeshi, Gujarati etc.) that just happen to be Muslim? It also makes it difficult for converts in the two keys areas of social activity and education.

If the local masjids are not up to scratch in terms of helping converts, converts have no option but to look elsewhere. They have to ask: who cares about us? Who cares about me?

This is where the charlatans and those like them step in, and they come in various shapes and sizes. Let us analyse them one by one:

1) Cults (Ar. *firaq*) and political activists, and what is meant by cults are organisations whose theological tenets do not match those of the orthodox, Sunni majority. As mentioned in the previous chapter, a lot of these organisations are proscribed in most of, if not all, of the Muslim world, and therefore they come to the Anglosphere and take advantage of the rights and freedoms that are available to them, e.g. speech, assembly etc.[17] The Muslim Brotherhood, especially in its modern, Salafized

---

[16] Have a look at this article as an example: http://www.myiwc.com/forums/showthread.php?t=6876 (Accessed Oct 11, 2016)
[17] Please see the New York Times article above.

form, is the most predominant of these organisations in the Anglosphere, especially the United Stated and the United Kingdom.[18]

I don't want to go into too much detail regarding cults and organisations like the Muslim Brotherhood, as there are far better books and even videos that deal with these topics. What I will say is this: look out for individuals and organisations that seek to waste your time. Once you have embraced Islam, you need to be studying and growing, which means theology, *fiqh*, basic Arabic and so forth. You also want to be around believers who will assist you in this development and growth. People who expect you to march and demonstrate on the streets for the sake of political causes, sometimes expecting you to travel for several hours to other cities and states, are people who will waste your time. These are the same people who regularly expect you to sign petitions, or send letters to members of Parliament or Congress.

If you feel you must, or you are just curious, go ahead and spend some time with these people and those who follow them. Do they study Islam in any systematic fashion? Are the people who follow them learning the basics of their *fiqh* and theology and moving through texts? Can they answer questions about Islam when

---

[18] For further details please see http://www.naseemalsham.com/en/Pages.php?page=readDynamicCom&id=52306&comid=96&name=Research%20and%20Articles&sub=Fat%C4%81w%C4%81%20that%20Appear%20Islamic%20But%20Actually%20Serve%20the%20West (Accessed Nov 30, 2016) as well as this documentary: https://www.youtube.com/watch?v=0E8_owx8qeE (Accessed Nov 30, 2016)

asked by a fellow Muslim, or when asked by an unbeliever? Is there any discernible development or growth in these people between when they first join and several months or even years later? If the answer is repeatedly 'no' then you know that these people are a waste of time.[19]

2) "Spiritual" organisations, also known as Sufi ṭarīqahs, and these are organisations that are ostensibly orthodox in terms of their theology but will place disproportionate emphasis on the purification of the heart, to the inevitable detriment of one's studies of theology and *fiqh*. Historically, these organisations were means of creating well-rounded Muslims, meaning that they were proficient theologically, legally and spiritually. Nowadays, these organisations are more like personality cults, in which the *shaykh*, or leader of the organisation, is the centre of attention and is held to be infallible and never questioned.

The sad result of this is that the followers of this *shaykh*, commonly known as *murīds*, do not develop in their faith, meaning that they do not study theology, fiqh, memorise any of the Qur'ān and so forth, even if they spend years in the organisation. However, they will be very good at quoting the *shaykh* on just about every issue, from spiritual matters all the way through to what school one should send one's kids to and who to vote for in an upcoming election.

---

[19] For more details on development and growth as a new Muslim, please see 'A Guide for New Believers' http://mahdinnm.blogspot.com/2011/05/guide-for-new-believers.html (accessed Nov 29, 2016)

Another problem that arises amongst the followers is self-satisfaction, in that they feel that merely being a follower of the *shaykh* is sufficient and there is no need to expend any further effort. The self-satisfaction can also lead to arrogance and snobbery, in which the followers of the *shaykh* display disdain and contempt towards those who are not followers, and sometimes this is encouraged by the *shaykh* himself. Non-followers are viewed as inexorably deficient and irredeemable.

The relationship between such a leader and his followers should really be like that of a boxer and a trainer. A trainer tells his boxer how to exercise, what kind of routine to have, what foods to eat and so forth, and at the end of the training it is the boxer who steps into the ring to fight his opponent. The sheikh of a ṭarīqah, likewise, is supposed to advise his followers on how to take care of themselves, how to better themselves as Muslims, which should include routine and diet, and how to prepare themselves for the constant fight against their egos, their desires, worldly temptations and Shayṭān. It is the follower that steps into the ring, or indeed is already in the ring, to fight against these enemies, not the sheikh. However, the impression one gets from many of these followers is that the sheikh is in the ring fighting on their behalf.

If you want to know whether a ṭarīqah is beneficial or not, you need to ask the same questions that you would ask of cults and political organisations. Are the followers developing or are they just staying the same, day after day, month after month, year after year?[20]

3) There is one more group that needs to be addressed, and this is probably the most important group of all. The abovementioned groups are easy to identify and thus avoid and circumvent, but this last group has no formal association between its major proponents and is very good at marketing itself as a reasonable alternative. I am talking about a group of people that I call the "hippie converts".

These are English-speaking converts who embraced Islam in the 1970s. As mentioned in the first episode of my podcast, The Foreword,[21] these people were "discovering themselves". They were looking for "truth" and "meaning" and exploring various religions, traditions and cultures, eventually settling on Islam. The question is: did these people become Muslim purely out of conviction or was it more to do with the zeitgeist of the time? For them, maybe being a Muslim meant being anti-establishment, being radical and being part of the counterculture.[22] Citing *The Autobiography of Malcolm X* as a major reason for conversion is

---

[20] For further details, please see this article: https://jurjis.wordpress.com/2011/01/26/our-failure-is-our-loss-2-peddling-purity/ (Accessed March 13, 2017)

[21] https://www.youtube.com/watch?v=2dkljTZpYqY&t (Accessed July 12, 2018)

[22] For more details: https://infogalactic.com/info/Counterculture_of_the_1960s (Accessed Nov 27, 2016)

indicative,[23] but this excerpt from a conversion story is quite clear:

"My mother went to Berkeley, and that says enough. She was very active in the civil rights movement. She took me when I was 12, to the Soledad Brother's (trial), to George Jackson's prison trial, just to see what was happening, that there were political struggles going on in this country.

She was very opposed to the Vietnam War. We grew up, with a lot of social awareness...my close family is wealthy, my particular family is not wealthy at all...But definitely the area we were in was quite wealthy. So, I think my Mother wanted to make sure that we understood that this country has a lot of inequities.

My sister was in Salma, Alabama marching ...that's the type background we were raised in. And the 60's was a fascinating time. Berkeley was right across the street, I grew up quite literally across the street...and we were aware that there were big things happening, in the states."[24]

Here is another example:

"I studied Zen Buddhism, Confucianism, and other eastern mystical traditions. I went on Arnold Ehret's mucousless diet for about six

---

[23] See this example: http://www.nawawi.org/?page_id=79 (Accessed Nov 27, 2016) Many converts to Islam in the United States did so after reading *The Autobiography of Malcolm X*. However, my question is about the primary motive: was it conviction that Islam is the truth or was it because they saw Islam as politically, socially or culturally revolutionary? If someone bases their conversion on *The Autobiography* but then decades later promotes and endorses *The Study Quran*, which more or less renders conviction in Islam meaningless, the indication is that such a person was more attracted to the political, social and cultural messages in *The Autobiography*, and Allah knows best.
[24] http://shaykhhamza.com/biography/ (Accessed Nov 27, 2016)

months, and for a period of about eighteen months I was an active practitioner of transcendental meditation.

For one reason or another, I found all of these paths unfulfilling. Finally, by mere chance, I happened to meet a fellow airman, who happened to be a Muslim. She had heard of my quest and gave me a copy of an Islamic book to read. In the pages of that volume I found what I had been looking for. Shortly thereafter, I converted to Islam.

That was my most formative religious experience. It helped me to understand and gracefully accept my mother's early demise. It provided me with the insight needed to reconcile with my father. It provided me with the spiritual path I had futilely sought in transcendental meditation. Finally, it has helped me to gradually overcome the baggage that comes with growing up as a racial minority in the American underclass, and it has helped to direct me towards a life of study and service to others."[25]

I hope the reader can see a trend. There is other stuff going on besides conviction. Someone coming from a Christian background, as is the case with the individuals quoted above, would be expected to believe in the existence of the Creator but maybe find something lacking or unclear in Christianity, especially the Trinitarian theology, and therefore moving towards Islam should be a natural progression. Are you looking for a direct relationship with your Lord, a relationship that is capable of being obtained and enjoyed regardless of one's rank

---

[25] http://www.mujahideenryder.net/2007/01/03/imam-zaid-shakirs-conversion-story/ (Accessed Nov 27, 2016)

within some clerical hierarchy? Are you looking for straightforward, uncomplicated, absolute monotheism?

Why would someone from a Christian background even consider Buddhism? What is their point of departure? Is it: 'I know God exists but I don't know what His true religion is', or is it something along the lines of 'I feel spiritually deficient and I need something spiritually fulfilling'?

I've worded these two points of departure very deliberately, because the difference should be obvious. Someone who becomes Muslim based on conviction does so because he is seeking the truth, regardless of what that truth is or how it makes him feel. The one seeking "spirituality" is looking for something to make him feel good.

Is the exploration of Buddhism and Confucianism and other eastern traditions part of the zeitgeist of that age? We have an answer:

"...This is 1977, probably '76, '77, prior to the Iranian Revolution and what was happening then. Islam is the last place that people look in the United States, traditionally. You'd look at Buddhism, Hinduism, probably Shintoism or Daoism, before someone would think about looking at Islam."[26]

---

[26] http://shaykhhamza.com/biography/2 (Accessed Nov 28, 2016)

Before continuing, I want to make it clear that what I've said and what I'm about to say is not meant to gainsay whatever benefit converts from that era have brought to Muslims in the Anglosphere and elsewhere. Rather, and this will be the ultimate conclusion of this book, we are seeking to establish where final authority in Islam lies, which is where every Muslim should invest his faith. There are plenty of Muslims who have knowledge, who can teach, who can translate, who can give a good lecture, but they are not worthy of being invested in wholeheartedly, and this is for two main reasons. The first is that they have not reached a level of knowledge in which they can be called an authority. The second is that they are still alive.

On my blog and in the introduction to my translation of Imam an-Nawawī's *Adāb al-ʿĀlim wa al-Mutaʿallim wa al-Muftī wa al-Mustaftī*,[27] al-Hajj Abū Jaʿfar al-Ḥanbalī explains how authority in Islam works and how authorities are identified,[28] but we want to focus on the idea of investing one's faith.

Think of your faith as the most precious thing you have, similar to your life's savings. If you lose it, you will be in serious trouble. How are you going to store your life's savings? Would you store them in Pakistani rupees, Euros, American dollars? The first currency is weak and unstable, so no. The Euro is a disaster waiting to happen, and has been that way ever since it was

---

[27] This translation has now been published: http://www.ibfim.com/img/kmc/2017-publications/007.jpg (Accessed Sept 26, 2017)

[28] http://mahdinnm.blogspot.com/2016/02/authority-in-islam.html (Accessed Nov 28,2016)

introduced. The American dollar is the world's reserve currency, but how long is that going to last? No paper currency remains the reserve currency forever. Is there anything else, any other monetary form?

What about gold? The value of gold is stable. It's not subject to inflation unless there is a highly rare mass discovery. Gold has also stood the test of time. It has been a safe haven for rulers, governments, wealthy elites and others for millennia. Gold would clearly be the best option.

What does it mean to invest your faith in gold? For us, gold is the scholars who have stood the test of time and whose value has never decreased. Think of someone like Imam an-Nawawī, may Allah have mercy on him, whose book is mentioned above. This is a scholar of remarkable authority. His books, especially in the sciences of fiqh and ḥadīth, continue to be studied and read to this day. His Lord called him home well over 700 years ago, which means that we know everything we are going to know about him and there are no surprises lurking in ambush.

If you invest your faith in Imam an-Nawawī and people like him, people who have stood the test of time and whose value has never decreased, your faith will be safe. If you turn to people like this for answers to your questions, for advice in difficult times, for guidance in the face of falsehood, you will be well-served, and your faith will be safe. It is these people that you need to look at and tell yourself, 'These are the people bearing Islam. Islam is with these people.'

When it comes to studying and learning from people who are alive, you want to be with those people who have saved the gold. You want to follow the living people who, in turn, follow the likes of Imam an-Nawawī in word, creed and deed. Living people like this are akin to a strong paper currency, and a strong paper currency is backed up by gold. They become gold themselves after they have left this world and their works and legacy have stood the test of time. Following people like this and benefitting from them is similar to having gold in one's vault while using cash for one's day to day transactions. No matter what happens to the cash, the gold is always there, safe and sound, ready to back you up.

In short, we judge the living by the dead.

The dangers of investing your faith entirely in living people, especially those who are not backed up by gold, should now be clear to you. If you look at a living person, or a group of living people, and tell yourself, 'These are the people bearing Islam. Islam is with these people', you are investing your life savings in paper currencies. Some are stronger than others, that's true, but none of them are gold, and they can he hyperinflated until they are worthless. If you invest your faith in some Sufi shaykh or hippie convert or cult or political organisation, what will happen when that individual or organisation disappoints you? What will happen to your faith when they drastically change course or can no longer meet your needs? You will lose your faith, plain and simple.

Let's go back to the hippie converts and why September 11th, 2001 was mentioned at the beginning of this book. It appears that, by and large, the hippie converts were attracted to Islam at that time because it was part of the counterculture and represented opposition to the establishment. It was exotic and romantic. It was trendy and hip to be a Muslim and this lasted all the way through to 2001. The release of Spike Lee's *Malcolm X* in 1992, which was critically acclaimed and nominated for prestigious awards, is further indication of this.

We can also look at the various radical and controversial statements that were made by several of these hippie converts in the years leading up to 2001[29] and then the drastic changes that were made afterwards. The events of September 11, 2001 were a very rude awakening, a realisation that it is not always cool and trendy to be a Muslim. As a Muslim, you are a person of the Hereafter in the world, surrounded by people of the world, and this means that you can never be reconciled to the world. Those who are reconciled to the world are in rebellion against Allah and His Messenger, may Allah bless him and grant him peace, and this is the vast majority of humanity.

Therefore, if you ever get the sense that being Muslim has made you "acceptable", or "trendy", or "interesting", know that this is

---

[29] For example: http://www.islamicpluralism.org/244/the-sufi-master-of-deceit-hamza-yusuf-hanson (Accessed Nov 29, 2016),

indeed a delusion and an emotional mirage. Either you are being lied to or you are being used, or both.[30]

The events of September 11, 2001 and what followed brought the realisation that not only was being a Muslim no longer exotic and trendy, it was also dangerous and risky. If you were a Muslim living in the Anglosphere, and especially the United States, many people now looked at you with suspicion and derision. You were now at risk of ending up in Guantanamo Bay, or maybe some other high-security prison. Expressing radical, anti-Western or anti-American views could now get you into serious trouble. As one of these prominent converts put it, the private and public discourse now had to be the same:

"That is what we find when we demystify power. A lot of it is just our own ignorance here. People need to hear the truth, but if you are harsh or hard-hearted, people will not listen to you. They will just flee from you. I think that we have allowed too much harshness into our discourse, and I can say that for my own self in some of the past talks I have given. We need to really rethink a lot about what we say in our discourses…

"That is why I think that if Muslims could get out there and just speak from the heart, it would make a real difference. I think duplicity is a really dangerous thing. Our public and private discourses have to be the same because one of the things they are trying to do now is

---

[30] For further details about how you can be used as a Muslim in the Anglosphere, please see my post on Cultural Marxism: http://mahdinnm.blogspot.com/2016/10/cultural-marxism.html (Accessed Nov 29, 2016),

undermine the public discourse of the Muslims. What they did to Dr. Siddiqi was really malignant because he was at the National Cathedral and gave that prayer, and he also met with President Bush, and they had him on Fox News from some old video saying that he supported Hizbullah and Hamas and things like that. Then they were calling him, "terrorist in the White House" and things like that. We are no longer in the little leagues anymore."[31]

As the prominent convert admitted, there was a lot of harshness in previous talks and lectures, and that was now going to be used as evidence of hostility towards the American government, American values or America in general. The discourse now had to change, or Muslims living there would find themselves faced with growing hostility from Americans and possibly legal troubles.

So how did the discourse change?

For starters, 2001 was the year that something called "Minority Fiqh", or "Fiqh of Minorities" achieved prominence in Europe and the Anglosphere, so much so that one of the preeminent authorities of Islam, Imam Muḥammad Saʿīd Ramaḍān al-Būṭī, may Allah have mercy on him, came out and spoke against it.[32] Two years later, while visiting France, he gave a more scathing

---

[31] www.muslimsforjesus.org/Current%20Affairs/America's%20Tragedy-An%20Islamic%20Perspective%20by%20Shayk%20Hamza%20Yusuf%20at%20the%20Zaytuna%20Institute.html (Accessed Nov 29, 2016)
[32] http://mahdinnm.blogspot.com/2011/01/fiqh-of-minorities-part-1.html (Accessed Nov 30, 2016)

and more detailed critique.[33] A year later, the CD set entitled *Sacred Law in Secular Lands* was released,[34] a full-blown endorsement and promotion of the very thing that Imam al-Būṭī had warned against.[35]

It is indeed ironic that my attention was brought to Imam al-Būṭī's pronouncements on Minority Fiqh by the very people who have been advocating it. After obtaining my degree in Arabic and History in 2004, I contacted a certain Islamic institute in California to offer my translation services. A representative for the institute in the United Kingdom replied and asked me to translate the two aforementioned pronouncements and informed me that they would be published online, on sites like masud.co.uk and Deenport.

I translated the first one, which predates the other and is shorter, had it checked by one of my teachers and then sent it off. It was never published on any of those sites. When I inquired, I was told that the head of the institute was 'looking at it'.

A few years later, in 2008, I got in touch with a website and publishing house who asked me to translate Imam al-Būṭī's

---

[33] http://mahdinnm.blogspot.com/2011/02/fiqh-of-minorities-part-2.html (Accessed Nov 30, 2016)
[34] https://www.amazon.com/Sacred-Law-Secular-Lands-Survival/dp/B000BHISB0 (Accessed Nov 30, 2016)
[35] For further details on what happened during those years and how it affected Anglosphere Islam, please read: http://mahdinnm.blogspot.com/2015/12/why-do-they-support-trump.html (Accessed Nov 30, 2016)

theology book, *Kubrā al-Yaqīniyyāt al-Kawniyyah*.[36] Seeing as the Imam's first pronouncement had not yet been published, I sent it across and it was posted on their website. The response, from online forums and elsewhere, was generally positive. I then decided to translate the second, lengthier pronouncement, and I included several explanatory footnotes.

The response to the second was not so positive. One of the teachers at the institute in California threatened to withdraw his endorsement of the website if certain footnotes were not removed. He couldn't say anything about the Imam's actual words, only that maybe the translation was possibly incorrect. The brothers who run the website unfortunately caved and removed the footnotes, but the original article with all the footnotes is still available on my blog.[37] A part of this teacher's endorsement reads, 'The site allows the reader to make his/her own decision as to what truly represents orthodox and traditional views on doctrine, law/practice, etc. by allowing one to reference the words of Muslim scholars deeply rooted in knowledge and esteemed highly throughout our history.'[38] The reader is allowed to do so as long as it does not make certain Muslims in the Anglosphere look bad.

---

[36] I started translating the book that year but then stopped and instead studied it with a teacher. I completed the translation in 2016 and it is now being published by Dār al-Fikr in Damascus.
[37] As of November 30, 2016, that same website has removed all articles by Imam al-Būṭī, which presumably has something to do with their stance on the foreign invasion of Syria. In addition to my blog, the two pronouncements are also available at www.naseemalsham.com.
[38] http://marifah.net/testimonials-mainmenu-67 (Accessed Nov 30, 2016)

This story should give you an idea of how Islam in the Anglosphere works, and there are more examples. Please understand that there is hustling going on. There are people who are making a comfortable living from giving lectures, "deen intensives" and generally giving empty platitudes when asked and paid to do so.[39]

The next step in changing the discourse was striving for unity with cults, especially the Salafis, and this culminated in the so-called "Salafi-Sufi unity pact" of 2007.[40] As can be seen from the text of the document, the importance of studying creed is downplayed, especially the beautiful and unique aspects of orthodox theology that display both its truth and majesty, such as salvation being by faith alone and not deeds, enjoying and relishing a direct relationship with one's Lord and the promise of seeing one's Lord in the Hereafter.[41]

If these matters are removed from the forefront of a believer's mind, his relationship with his Lord will be hindered and hampered. Salvation being by faith alone and not deeds means that you do not worship Allah in order to be saved but you worship Allah because you *are* saved. He has granted you

---

[39] Here is an example of Anglosphere Salafis admitting to the problem in their own ranks: http://www.islam21c.com/islamic-thought/muslim-speakers-dawah-money/ (Accessed Nov 30, 2016)
[40] https://www.newislamicdirections.com/nid/articles/pledge_of_mutual_respect_and_cooperation_between_sunni_muslim_scholars_orga/ (Accessed Nov 30, 2016)
[41] For further details, please see http://mahdinnm.blogspot.com/2010/12/purpose-of-life.html (Accessed Nov 30, 2016)

salvation, as a free gift from Him, and therefore every act of worship and obedience that you perform is actually an expression of gratitude.

Imam an-Nawawī, may Allah have mercy on him, in his commentary on the first ḥadīth in his famous collection of forty ḥadīth, quotes another ḥadīth in which ʿĀʾishah, may Allah be pleased with her, the Mother of the Believers and wife of the Messenger of Allah, may Allah bless him and grant him peace, sees her husband praying at night until his ankles have become swollen. She then asks him why he does this when Allah has forgiven him for anything he could have done and anything he could possibly do. His response was simple yet profoundly beautiful, {Should I not be a grateful slave?} May Allah raise both the writer and the reader to a state in which all worship is seen as an expression of gratitude, āmīn!

Having a direct relationship with Allah is what sets us apart from the Jews and the Christians. There is no high priest who enters the temple, goes behind the curtain, and speaks to the Lord directly on behalf of the rest of the congregation. Ibn Shihāb az-Zuhrī, the great scholar of ḥadīth and the Prophetic biography (d.124 AH), said, 'Raising the hands[42] is symbolic of lifting the veil between a person and his Lord.'[43]

---

[42] i.e. at the beginning of the prayer
[43] This is quoted by Imam ʿAlāʾ ad-Din al-Mardāwī in his book al-Inṣāf fī Maʿrifat ar-Rājiḥ min al-Khilāf. Please see al-Muqniʿ wa ash-Sharḥ al-Kabīr wa Mahima al-Inṣāf (Giza: Hajr, 1414/1993), p.421

As for the bountiful gift of seeing Allah in the Hereafter, Imam ash-Shafiʿi's words on the matter, as quoted by Imam al-Būṭī in his theology book, suffice:

Al-Rabīʿ, may Allah have mercy on him, mentioned that he was with al-Shāfiʿī one day when a letter came from Upper Egypt in which the writer was asking about His statement, Mighty and Majestic is He: "No indeed! Rather that Day they will be veiled from their Lord." [al-Muṭaffifīn 83:15] He wrote in response, 'Some people being veiled out of His wrath indicates that some people will see Him out of His pleasure.' Al-Rabīʿ said to him, 'Is this what you believe, my master?' He replied, 'By Allah, if Muḥammad ibn Idrīs were not absolutely certain that he was going to see his Lord in the Hereafter, he would not worship Him in this life.'[44]

Pay attention, keep your eyes and ears open, and you will notice that no one in the Anglosphere, especially the hippie converts and their affiliates, will publicly speak about the three aforementioned matters.[45] Maybe it is for the sake of "unity" and they do not want to offend the cultists that they meet from time to time, or maybe they are not so convinced of such matters themselves. Allah knows best. One hippie convert, on a blog that was administered by *Newsweek* and *The Washington Post* and has since been taken down, was even questioned by a Christian about how a Muslim has a direct relationship with the Lord, because he simply did not see it. The comment had been on the blog for

---

[44] *Kubrā al-Yaqīniyyāt al-Kawniyyah* (Damascus: Dār al-Fikr, 2008) p. 173
[45] i.e. salvation being by faith alone, having a direct relationship with the Lord, and seeing the Lord in the Hereafter.

months when I first read it and no answer had been provided by the hippie convert.

The third major event that changed the discourse is something called the Mardin Declaration, which is the conclusion of a conference that was held in Mardin, Turkey in 2010. The official website has since been taken down, but the full document is still available on the official website of its chief proponent.[46] In summary, the conference drew the conclusion that the classic terms Dār al-Islām (i.e. the Abode of Islam) and Dār al-Kufr (i.e. the Abode of Unbelief) no longer applied, and all of this was based on a complete distortion and twisting of a *fatwā* by Imam Taqī ad-Dīn Ibn Taymiyyah.[47]

Without going into too much detail as a thorough refutation of the conference is in the footnotes, a few main points should be stressed. Please have a look at this statement, quoted directly from the official website of the chief proponent:

'The classification of abodes in Islamic jurisprudence was a classification based on *ijtihad* (juristic reasoning) that was necessitated by the circumstances of the Muslim world, then and the nature of the international relations prevalent at that time. However, circumstances have changed now: The existence of recognized international treaties,

---

[46] Please see http://binbayyah.net/arabic/archives/1038 (Accessed Dec 1, 2016)
[47] Imam Taqī ad-Dīn Ibn Taymiyyah is a Ḥanbalī scholar and jurist, yet not a single Ḥanbalī scholar was present at this conference, i.e. someone qualified to explain what the *fatwā* means and how it is to be treated. For a thorough refutation from the Ḥanbalī side, please see this: https://jurjis.wordpress.com/2011/04/02/mardin-fatwa-madness-and-muffling-falsehood-1abujafaral-hanbali/ (Accessed Dec 1, 2016)

which consider as crimes wars that do not involve repelling aggression or resisting occupation; the emergence of civil states which guarantee, on the whole, religious, ethnic and national rights, have necessitated declaring, instead, the entire world as a place of tolerance and peaceful co-existence between all religions, groups and factions in the context of establishing common good and justice amongst people, and wherein they enjoy safety and security with respect to their wealth, habitations and integrity. This is what the Shari'ah has been affirming and acknowledging, and to which it has been inviting humanity, ever since the Prophet (peace and blessings be upon him) migrated to Madina and concluded the first treaty/peace agreement that guaranteed mutual and harmonious co-existence between the factions and various ethnic/race groups in a framework of justice and common/shared interest. Shortcomings and breaches perpetrated by certain states that happen to scar and mar this process cannot and should not be used as a means for denying its validity and creating conflict between it and the Islamic Shari'ah.'[48]

This is only one portion of the document and a book could be written on the falsehoods it contains, as stated in the refutation cited above. The classification of abodes in Islamic law is not simply a matter of *ijtihād* but is in the Qur'ān itself in Sūrat an-Nisā', the fourth chapter, verse 97: **"The angels ask those who they take while they are wronging themselves, 'What were your circumstances?' They reply, 'We were oppressed on earth.' They say, 'Was Allah's earth not wide enough for you to have made Hijrah (i.e. to have migrated) elsewhere in it?' The shelter of such people will be Hell. What an evil destination!"**

---

[48] http://binbayyah.net/arabic/archives/1038 (Accessed Dec 1, 2016)

Making Hijrah, or migrating, requires a place of departure and a place of arrival. In this verse, what place are these people supposed to be leaving and where are they supposed to be going? They are supposed to be leaving Dār al-Kufr for Dār al-Islām.[49]

Read further and the errors become more egregious. The document states that the division of the earth into abodes no longer applies because circumstances have changed, and circumstances have changed because of "recognised international treaties". Amazingly, this is exactly what Imams like Wahbah az-Zuḥaylī and Muḥammad Saʿīd Ramaḍān al-Būṭī, may Allah have mercy on both of them, were warning about in the 1960s, almost fifty years prior to the conference.[50]

The rest of the segment states that these treaties guarantee safety and security for all of humanity, and this is what the Revealed Law of Islam has always affirmed. Therefore, and this is not made explicit in the text, there really is no need to make any effort for serious change in the world. The way it is now is what Allah is pleased with. In terms of governance and rulership, everything that needs to be put in place is already there. The whole world is, effectively, Dār al-Islam. We can all go home now.

---

[49] Please see this article for further details on the subject: http://mahdinnm.blogspot.com/2011/04/abodes-of-earth.html (Accessed Dec 1, 2016)

[50] Please see this article for further details on the subject: http://mahdinnm.blogspot.sg/2016/10/religion-of-peace.html?m=0 (Accessed Dec 1, 2016)

But why, then, is Imam al-Mahdī going to come? What exactly is he going to rectify? What about the False Messiah, al-Masīḥ ad-Dajjāl? I thought his followers were already building a system for him to inherit when he appears on earth. What about the second coming of 'Īsā, peace be upon him? Is he going to come down, give a thumbs-up and then go back to Allah?

The official website for the Mardin Declaration has been taken down, which might be a good sign, but to this day none of the attendees or advocates have publicly renounced it or absolved themselves of it.

The fourth and final major change in the discourse is the hippie convert endorsement and promotion of a treacherous "translation" of the Qur'ān known as *The Study Quran*, which is essentially a new interpretation of Allah's Book based on the perennialist school. Just as there are countless books out there that would be detrimental for a Muslim to read, there are countless books about Islam in particular and interpretations of Allah's Book that would be detrimental for Muslims to read, but if orthodox Muslims in general are not aware of them and are not reading them, there is no need to warn against them, as this would draw unnecessary attention to them and most likely cause more harm than benefit. This was the whole point of the article that was written in early 2016 by Abū Nur al-Mizzī.[51]

---

[51] http://mahdinnm.blogspot.com/2016/01/the-accommodation-and-promotion-of.html (Accessed Dec 2, 2016)

The article was not written to refute perennialism per se but to refute the promotion and accommodation of it by people who are supposed to be Sunnis. The main point of contention with perennialism is that it advocates the validity of other religions, i.e. that they are true and valid paths to salvation, which is blatant heresy and a complete contradiction of what is found in the Book and the Sunnah and what all the scholars have made consensus on.[52]

There are other decent interpretations of the Qur'ān in English, such as the one by Marmaduke Pickthall or *The Noble Qur'an* by Abdalhaqq and Aisha Bewley, which relies on authoritative, orthodox commentaries such as those by Imams Ibn Juzayy al-Kalbī, al-Qurṭubī and Abū Bakr Ibn al-ʿArabī. The language is not archaic, like many other interpretations, and thus it is very accessible and digestible. Why this interpretation[53] was never promoted and endorsed in the way *The Study Quran* has been is a mystery. These hippie converts are supposed to have, at least on paper, the same theology as the Bewleys, not the theology of the perennialists, or maybe it is the theology of the perennialists that they have since adopted.

---

[52]Please see this article for further details: https://www.safinasociety.org/uploads/4/8/2/3/48238467/first_pillar_part_i_-_thirty_verses_on_the_soteriological_exclusivity_of_islam.pdf (Accessed Dec 2, 2016) This article is also beneficial: https://www.safinasociety.org/uploads/4/8/2/3/48238467/first_pillar_part_ii_universal_validity_of_religions_in_the_sq.pdf (Accessed Dec 2, 2016)
[53] I prefer this term as there can never be a real translation of the Qur'ān. Please see the fatwa on the following page.

Promoting and endorsing such a book is unlawful and sinful, as the authorities have declared.[54] One has to ask: what is the point? Are they trying to create a new Islam? Are they trying to create an Anglosphere or American Islam? The promotion and endorsement of *The Study Quran* has to be seen in light of the three previous monstrosities, because there is a clear pattern. Minority Fiqh devalued Islam in general and *fiqh* in particular by allowing for Islam to be subsumed and devoured by American and European culture. Struggling to implement your faith in certain parts of the world no longer meant that you had to move to where you could. Instead, you could just reconcile to the world, using the excuse that you are part of a minority.

The "unity pact" of 2007 devalued orthodox, Sunni Islam, and the beauties of our theology, as explained above. Studying theology in any depth so as to draw closer to Allah through knowing Him was discouraged.

The Mardin Declaration devalued, or indeed rendered meaningless, any effort to establish justice on earth or just to make the world a better place. Instead, the way the world is now is what Allah is pleased with. There's nothing more for us to do.

The promotion and endorsement of *The Study Quran* looks like the final nail in the coffin. The first three monstrosities render living as a Muslim in this world utterly meaningless; the last one renders being a Muslim for the sake of one's Hereafter equally

---

[54] Please see this fatwa: http://mahdinnm.blogspot.com/2016/04/fatwa-on-study-quran.html (Accessed Dec 2, 2016)

meaningless. There is nothing left worth living for and nothing left worth dying for.

Back in 2006, after the Danish cartoon incident, one of the hippie converts talked about "going it alone", i.e. letting Islam in the West break off from Islam in the East:

'Whatever we do, as Muslims in the West, we may be approaching the day when we will have to go it alone. If our coreligionists in the East cannot respect the fact that we are trying to accomplish things here in the West, and that their oftentimes ill-considered actions undermines that work in many instances, then it will be hard for us to consider them allies.'[55]

But what are they trying to accomplish? Allah knows best, but it looks like they are trying to establish an Islam that is unique for the Anglosphere, or America in particular, and in order to do so they have to break ranks with the authorities of Islam in the Muslim heartlands. In order for Islam to be established in America, or enfranchised, as they like to say, it has to follow the path of other religious groups, especially the Catholics.[56] This means that Islam will have to be compartmentalised and subjugated to the values of America.[57]

---

[55] https://www.newislamicdirections.com/nid/articles/clash_of_the_uncivilised (Accessed Dec 2, 2016)
[56] http://www.csmonitor.com/Commentary/Opinion/2010/0916/Amid-mosque-dispute-Muslims-can-look-to-Irish-Catholics-for-hope (Accessed Dec 2, 2016)
[57] Please see this video by Judge Andrew Napolitano: https://www.youtube.com/watch?v=_Vpqw0f2xbg and this article:

The conclusion of these four monstrosities is that American Islam is not Islam at all. It is completely devoid of objective standards[58] and is thus nothing more than a knockdown counterfeit. Furthermore, it is detached from the authorities of Islam, having cut itself adrift, and Allah knows best where it is headed. The importance of authorities, identifying them and benefiting from them will be discussed in the next chapter.

http://mahdinnm.blogspot.com/2015/09/ben-carson-is-right.html (Accessed Dec 2, 2016)
[58] Please see this article for further details: http://mahdinnm.blogspot.com/2016/01/the-importance-of-objective-standards.html (Accessed Dec 2, 2016)

Chapter 4: The Importance of the Arabic Language and Travelling to the Muslim World

"We have made it an Arabic Qur'ān so that hopefully you will use your intellect." [az-Zukhruf' 43:3]

Without the Arabic language, your Islam will always be deficient. There is no nice way of saying this. Arabic is the language of the Qur'ān, the language of the Sunnah and the language of well over 99% of all Islamic literature. No other language, be it Persian, Turkish, Urdu or English, comes anywhere close. Without it, you are dependent on translations and translators and you will never have access to original sources. This will make you easy prey for the people and organisations mentioned in the previous chapter. You did not become a Muslim so that you could be spiritually hustled and pimped. Whatever street smarts you had before Islam, you need not only to hang on to them after becoming Muslim but to hone them.

The great Imam ash-Shāfi'ī, may Allah be pleased with him, in his famous book *ar-Risālah*, states, 'It is an obligation upon every Muslim to learn whatever he is able to of the tongue of the Arabs, such that he can testify that there is no god but Allah and that Muḥammad is His Slave and His Messenger, that He can recite the Book of Allah, that he can articulate the invocations that are incumbent upon him, such as the *takbīr*,[59] and what is

---

[59] i.e. saying *Allahu Akbar* at the beginning of the prayer

commanded of him, such as the *tasbīḥ*,[60] the *tashahhud*[61] and so forth.'[62]

The Imam then says, 'And whoever increases in knowledge of the tongue that Allah made the tongue of he who is the seal of His Prophets and in which He sent down the last of His Books, that is better for him.'[63]

Learning Arabic has to be a priority alongside learning your basic theology and *fiqh*. You must learn at least enough so that you can perform your prayers properly, which will require you to recite portions of the Qur'ān and other invocations and supplications. I am not asking you to be hard on yourself or push yourself beyond your capacity. Do whatever you are capable of doing but be persistent. As the Messenger of Allah, may Allah bless him and grant him peace, has told us, the most beloved of actions to Allah are those that are consistent, even if small.[64] Actions like this are more effective. If you were to pour a bucket of water over a rock, it would just wash off. However, if you were to let the same amount of water slowly drip onto the rock, it would eventually make a dent. Be consistent, even if it is just a little bit every day.[65]

---

[60] i.e. saying *Subḥān Allah*, or 'Glory be to Allah'
[61] i.e. the invocations that are said while sitting in prayer
[62] Muḥammad ibn Idrīs ash-Shāfiʿī, *ar-Risālah* (Beirut: Dar an-Nafaes, 1431/2010), p.53
[63] Ibid., p.54
[64] This ḥadīth is found in *al-Jāmiʿ as-Ṣaḥīḥ* of Imam al-Bukhārī
[65] Another analogy would be to think of stepping stones across a river. You have to step on every stone with both of your feet, not moving on to the next

Learning Arabic in the Anglosphere, or outside of the Arab world, is possible to a certain extent. You can certainly learn the alphabet, how to write letters to form words, how to read the Qurʾān and what you need to recite in prayer, and whatever else is of that approximate level. You just need a decent teacher and some effort.

As for taking your Arabic language to the next level, such that you will not only be comfortable in conversation but more importantly with reading Islamic texts, translating them and developing your knowledge, travelling to the Arab world is indispensable. Being in an environment in which Arabic is written everywhere, which is more important than the spoken element, is incredibly beneficial. Your brain will constantly be in a state of Arabic awareness, noticing Arabic letters, words and expressions and trying to comprehend them. Furthermore, if you find yourself in a country where English is barely spoken, you will be forced to speak Arabic, even if it is broken and even if it is not the dialect of that particular country.

The above is the benefit of just being there, and if you get the chance just to visit an Arab country, even if only for a few weeks or days, go for it. However, for greater benefit, try to stay longer and try to take some Arabic classes while you are there, or a full

stone until both your feet are firmly on the current one. In other words, only after you've consolidated your position in one stage can you look towards the next. Stepping stones tend to be wet and slippery, so if you rush it's most likely that you will slip and fall into the river, or you might find yourself struggling to maintain your balance on a specific stone, in which case you will need to step back, consolidate your position and then try again.

course in Arabic, preferably with an Arab who will only speak Arabic in class. The longer you stay the better, e.g. a month, a few months, or even an academic year.

An academic year, consisting of approximately twenty hours in class each week, should suffice if you put the effort in. In terms of effort, I would recommend what I call the three-peat method, which means that you go over material (grammar, vocabulary etc.) three times, once before class, once during class and once after class, which should usually be the homework that your teacher assigns. If you know that in your next class you are going to go over a vocabulary list, a grammar rule, a text, or all three, study all of them prior to the class by copying them out, and by hand. This will force your brain to concentrate. You do not want to be taken by surprise in the class. You want everything to be familiar. As for the text, copying that by hand will improve both your reading and your writing, as it will force your brain to think in Arabic. Your brain will get used to the way Arabic is expressed and composed, and thus when you write, it will come across as Arabic, or closer to Arabic, and not Arablish.

If Allah so wills, if you can get into such a routine, you will be well on the way to learning this amazing and blessed language. If you ever feel yourself losing motivation, visit a local library or bookstore and pick up one of the great books written by our galaxy of scholars. Try to read whatever of it you can, and whatever you cannot, because you do not know what it means, use that to motivate you to learn more and strive harder. These scholars are the people you want to spend your time with. These are the people you want to keep you company when you feel that you have no one else, when you feel there is no one else to answer your questions or simply to guide you and inspire you. Last and certainly not least, supplicate to Allah constantly. Ask Him to place a burning desire inside of you to learn the Arabic language and to allow you to use that language to learn His religion. At first, it will feel like you are pushing a boulder up a hill, or that the language is running away from you, but keep pushing. Eventually, you will feel yourself reaching the top of that hill, after which the boulder rolls nicely and gently along, and with Allah alone is every success.

As your Arabic studies in the Arab world continue, you will most likely notice certain things around you, and what I'm about to say would also apply to non-Arabic speaking parts of the Muslim world to a considerable extent. What you should notice is that Islam in these countries just *is*, and the Muslims there *live* it and *do* it. There are masjids and the Muslims pray there five times a day. People take time off on Friday, or even the whole day, to attend the Jumu'ah prayer. Both Eids are national holidays. Timetables and schedules are altered in Ramaḍān to accommodate fasting and breaking the fast at sunset. The meat in restaurants and shops is halal. Have you noticed that all of these things are matters that are frequently complained about in the Anglosphere?

Furthermore, there will be a lot of uniformity and harmony. Ramadan will start and end on the same day for everyone. Congregational prayers will be at the same time in every masjid. In the better countries of the Arab and Muslim world, there will even be study circles in masjids. No one in these countries *identifies*[66] as a Muslim. These people just *are* Muslims, even if outwardly it does not *look* that way.

Take Morocco as an example, which is probably the safest and most stable of any Arab or Muslim country. The ruling dynasty has been in power for well over three centuries. A typical Moroccan, man or woman, might not *look* very Muslim or Islamic, but a typical Moroccan, from the housemaid or worker in a souvenir shop to banker or university professor, knows the crucial and important basics of his faith. From my experience, every Moroccan knows that salvation is by faith alone and not deeds, and that they are going into Paradise because of Allah's mercy, not because of their deeds. Maybe Moroccans, and Allah knows best, do rely a bit much on Allah's mercy, but at least they know that His mercy exceeds His wrath. They know the sublime value of being Muslim and where they are going after they die.[67]

Compare this basic knowledge of Islam with that of Muslims in the Anglosphere. Even the so-called scholars, or spokesmen for Islam in the Anglosphere, will never, ever talk about faith-based salvation, even if you ask them to. The result is that Muslims are unaware of this immense gift, and when asked by a Christian missionary, for example, 'If you die tonight, where are you going?', they don't know how to answer. They're not convinced

---

[66] For example, like these poor people: http://www.mpvusa.org/mpv-principles/ (Accessed Dec 3, 2016). You can also listen to the podcast 'Islam as an Identity: https://www.youtube.com/watch?v=nXRt0b1a3FA&t (Accessed July 12, 2018)
[67] For a detailed elucidation of this crucial matter, please listen to the podcast entitled 'Salvation Is By Faith Alone, Not Deeds': https://www.youtube.com/watch?v=8npzB9cQ2_M (Accessed July 12, 2018)

of their own salvation. They believe they have to be that 51% good Muslim to have any hope of being saved, which is complete blasphemy.[68] Allah creates your deeds and gives you the ability to carry them out, so how can you *earn* Paradise by offering your deeds to Allah?

Like the example given in the article cited above, think of a father and his son. The father sees a homeless man so he says to his son, 'Take this change and give it to that man.' The boy takes the change, gives it to the man and then goes back to his father, at which the point the father says, 'Good boy'. Look at the situation again. Whose idea was it to give money to the homeless man? Whose money was given? The only thing the son did was obey his father. Does his father *owe* him anything for this good deed?

The truth is that the boy would not and could not have done that deed without his father, and this is how our relationship with our Lord is. He gives us everything; without Him we are nothing. The only thing we do is obey or disobey. To believe that you can *earn* Paradise through your works, meaning that Allah *owes* it to you because of your deeds, is idolatry.

Rather, the more good deeds we do, the more grateful we need to be, because who gives us the ability to perform good deeds? Then, once we have expressed gratitude, we need to thank Allah for our gratitude. Imam ash-Shāfiʿī, in the second line of his book *ar-Risālah*, says, 'Praise be to Allah, Who is not shown

---

[68] Please see this as a typical example: https://carm.org/can-muslim-do-enough-good-works-go-paradise (Dec 3, 2016)

gratitude for one of His blessings except through another blessing from Him, which in turn constitutes a new blessing for the one who has enjoyed those previous blessings and thus he must show gratitude for it.'[69]

You can never repay Allah for His favours. All you can do is obey and be grateful, and be grateful for your obedience and gratitude.

The creedal matter discussed above is so crucial and yet so simple, but it is lost on Anglosphere Muslims. Does one have to learn Arabic or travel to the Muslim world to learn these things, and learn them from common believers, not even theologians?

As mentioned above, there is a lot of hustling going on in the Anglosphere. There are people who are using Islam to make money. In order to create a steady income, a dependency culture has to be established. Certain individuals and organisations will present themselves to you as your only source of knowledge and information. Once you have completed a weekend course, or a "Deen intensive" or a "spiritual retreat", or a "knowledge retreat" with "some of the leading scholars of our time",[70] you will be expected to come back for more. Don't fall for it.

In the authentic collection of Imam al-Bukhārī, may Allah be pleased with him, the Messenger of Allah, may Allah bless him

---

[69] *Ar-Risālah*, p.26
[70] I'm not making this up: http://ummah.events/RISconvention/ris-knowledge-retreat-2017 (Accessed July 13, 2018) You can also read this article: http://mahdinnm.blogspot.com/2016/01/the-importance-of-objective-standards.html (Accessed July 13, 2018)

and grant him peace, says, {The most beloved of actions to Allah are the most consistent of them, even if small.} In the aforementioned example, water poured over a rock will just wash off. Water slowly dripped onto a rock will eventually make a dent. This is how your learning should be. If you attend a class every day, even half an hour, or less, or a class once a week for an hour or two, and you keep up with it for weeks and months, you will see benefit. You will see progress. This is because studying your faith will be incorporated into your life. It will be a part of your routine.

On the other hand, if studying your faith is not a regular feature of your life and after several months, or even years, you plunge into a week-long "intensive" course, what will the long-term benefit be? Yes, you will have had an "experience",[71] you will walk away with "memories", but how will it affect your life on a daily basis from now on? Most likely, you will return to your hometown feeling forlorn and crestfallen. You were just in a wonderfully spiritual environment and now you're back in the world, the *dunyā*!

Don't worry. This is exactly how the organisers of such retreats and courses want you to feel. They want you to come back for more, because when you do, it will be a few more thousand dollars in their coffers, so that you can *feel* great. In essence, what you're paying for is a spiritual high, after which you will crash

---

[71] "Experience of a lifetime" is the common expression used in trailers and promotional videos.

down and then some time later you will want another fix. This is how they create dependency.

These courses and retreats also place in your subconscious the notion that Islam cannot be fully enjoyed and relished in the "world". It cannot be truly savoured unless you are in some pristine, sterilised environment. Thus, when you leave the course or retreat and return to your hometown, you will have this lingering feeling of inadequacy, as if you're not meant to be there. Your Islam will always be inadequate and lacking as long as you are outside of that special environment.

Travelling to learn Arabic is not the same thing. For starters, you will be in the world, so to speak, while you are attending classes and doing whatever you need to outside of them. Unless you're going to the deserts of Mauritania or Yemen, don't expect it to be a pristine, sterilised environment. Dār al-Islām has its sinners and its rebels, especially in the larger cities. You will still see and hear plenty that will not please you, but this is the world. It is not a utopia and was never meant to be. Paradise is in the next life. Secondly, your study of the Arabic language for that specific period of time will not be intended as a spiritual high. Rather, it is a stepping stone, so that once you are back in your hometown you can continue with private studies and hopefully meeting a teacher on a regular basis. The trip should assist you in incorporating the study of Arabic, and the religion in general, into your life.

An Arabic course is also focused on the subject of Arabic and your level of progress, especially if you are in a small class or have one-on-one sessions. Your individual needs will be met to a far greater extent and you should expect to be in class for only a few hours every day. Courses and retreats designed in the Anglosphere tend to ram in several subjects over a short period of time, with several hours of classes every day, in addition to talks, lectures, presentations and other activities. Have you ever tried eating an apple in one bite?

In your hometown, whether you've been out to the Arab world or not, and you're looking for a teacher, try to find someone who has studied for several years in the Arab and Muslim world. On top of that, you should look for the following qualities, based on what a teacher should be doing once they arrive back in their hometown or native country.

The first step is giving talks and lectures. This is how a teacher announces his arrival after several years abroad. Think of someone lighting a fire in the desert; all sorts of people will show up to see what the fuss is all about, and maybe to warm their hands. After a while, a smaller group of people will ask the teacher, who at this stage is merely a speaker or lecturer, about doing something more serious, like a course. Warming their hands is fine and dandy, but are there no marshmallows? This will mean a weekend course or maybe a weekly class in which a specific topic can be covered, such as the attributes of Allah or the rulings for fasting the month of Ramaḍān. The third step occurs when an even smaller group of people ask about meat. This means studying books with the teacher, cover to cover, and then getting licensed by the teacher to teach them. It is these students that the teacher uses to reproduce himself, i.e. create more teachers who can then benefit more people in the community. The first teacher can then focus on these more advanced students while the advanced students teach those at the lower levels. A system is in place.

If someone graduated from a seminary or returned from their studies abroad ten, twenty, thirty years ago, or even more, and they're still on the speaker tour, something is wrong, and especially if they're collecting honoraria. Where are their students, those whom they have taught books to from cover to cover? It is a very common occurrence in the Anglosphere, especially amongst Pakistanis, to see someone referred to as a "scholar" but what they really mean is that the individual is a great orator and maybe a great debater. The individual in question will not have a single student[72] to his name. In fact, he might not even teach at all or put himself in a situation where he has to take questions from an audience. Instead, he gives a talk, entertains the crowd, collects his fee and goes home. When he dies, there will hardly be any legacy left behind.

A scholar has students and a scholar of higher calibre writes books, in Arabic. Arabic was once the lingua franca of the entire Muslim world, even in places like Turkey and the Indian subcontinent. If you were to survey the contributions of non-Arab nations to the Ummah of Islam, you would notice that non-Arabs a) learned the Arabic language, and to a very high level of proficiency and b) they wrote memorable works in Arabic that are

---

[72] i.e. a someone who has read at least one book with the teacher from cover to cover.

still read and respected centuries later. For example, the six most famous ḥadīth collections were all compiled by non-Arabs. Imam al-Bukhārī, as the name indicates, was from modern-day Uzbekistan. Imam Muslim was from Nishapur. Imam Abū Ḥanīfah, the compiler and codifier of what became the Ḥanafī legal school, was Persian, as was Imam Abū Ḥāmid al-Ghazālī, author of the great *Iḥyāʾ ʿUlūm ad-Dīn*. The primary Arabic grammar text taught in prestigious Islamic universities like al-Azhar in Cairo and al-Qarawiyyīn in Fes is *al-Ājurūmiyyah*, written by Abū ʿAbdillāh ibn Muḥammad ibn Dāwūd al-Ṣanhājī, known as Ibn Ājurūm, a Berber from Morocco who died in 723 AH. Some of the great commentaries[73] and supercommentaries[74] in Shāfiʿī *fiqh* are written by scholars from Java, in modern-day Indonesia, such as Imam Muḥammad Nawawī al-Jāwī's commentary on the text *Safīnat an-Najāḥ* and the seven-volume supercommentary on Imam Ibn Ḥajar's *al-Manhaj al-Qawīm* by al-ʿAlāmah at-Tarmasī, known simply as Ḥāshiyat at-Tarmasī. I bought my copy of the latter after it was highly recommend by Sheikh Muḥammad Tawfīq Ramaḍān al-Būṭī, a Kurdish scholar in Damascus and son of Imam Muḥammad Saʿīd Ramaḍān al-Būṭī,[75] whose written legacy includes a masterpiece in almost every science. In the Mālikī school, one simply cannot ignore the massive contribution of Africans, such as Imam ʿUthmān Dan

---

[73] Ar. *sharḥ*, pl. *shurūḥ*
[74] Ar. *ḥāshiyah*, pl. *hawāshī*
[75] He is now buried in Damascus next to Imam Ṣalāḥ ad-Dīn al-Ayyūbī (known as Saladin in the Anglosphere), another Kurd, who, in addition to being an outstanding military and political leader, was also a theologian and jurist and founded several seminaries throughout the Levant and Egypt.

Fodio, a prolific scholar who founded a caliphate in modern-day Nigeria in 1804 CE. It lasted one hundred years.

I think you get the picture. Throughout Islamic history, non-Arabs have learned the Arabic language, mastered the sciences of the Revealed Law, become scholars in their own right and then contributed to the scholarly tapestry of Islam by writing masterpieces in Arabic and also founding seminaries and universities, both in the Arab world and in their own homelands.

English-speaking Muslims, while often claiming that they will lead the impending revival of Islam, have not followed the same course, not in the least. For starters, how do so-called scholars in the Anglosphere compare to those in the Muslim heartlands? Have any of them written a book in Arabic that the rest of the Ummah can benefit from? Have they built seminaries and universities that are producing scholars and theologians on a regular basis?

The defense given is "the day and age we live in", or the fact that English-speaking Muslims live in Dār al-Kufr while all the other peoples mentioned above reside in Dār al-Islam, and it has been that way for centuries. The circumstances are different, meaning more difficult.

This argument is weak because you can't have it both ways. English-speaking "scholars" cannot be branded as "some of the leading scholars of our time" and then at the same time use the excuse of living in Dār al-Kufr for not accomplishing what scholars in the Muslim heartlands have achieved. We don't even have to look back at history; we can actually look at scholars and imams who have died in the past few years, such as Muḥammad Saʿīd Ramaḍān al-Būṭī or Wahbah az-Zuḥaylī. As mentioned above, the former has a modern masterpiece in almost every Islamic science. He also taught various sciences at the University of Damascus, taught privately at home and taught his own books to the general public at Masjid al-Īmān in Damascus. The latter, also a professor at the University of Damascus, wrote a seventeen-volume commentary on the Qurʾān and a thirteen-volume comparative *fiqh* book, as well as a two-volume *fiqh* book for each of the four schools. His books on *uṣūl al-fiqh*, or Islamic jurisprudence, are taught throughout the Muslim world, even in the Qarawiyyin University in Fes, and there are several more books that I don't have the time and space to mention here. These are just two stars from the galaxy of scholars that have come out of Syria, living a great deal of their lives under the Assad family dictatorship. These are scholars in the truest sense; they have both left behind considerable legacies, in the form of books and in the form of students.[76]

It is people like the two imams mentioned above that you want to have access to, as well as, of course, the great imams of the past, but when dealing with contemporary theological and legal issues, issues that imams of the past may not have dealt with or only referred to in brief, you need to have access to scholars who have studied and looked into these issues firsthand, drawn conclusions and can thus convey that knowledge to the entire Ummah in the

---

[76] Imam al-Būṭī also has a huge recorded legacy, i.e. recordings of his lessons and sermons. Please see www.naseemalsham.com.

present.[77] It is scholars like these who warned about the travesties of Minority Fiqh and the Mardin Declaration decades before they came to fruition.

In short, you want to have access to the authorities.[78] Knowledge of the Arabic language and experience of living in the Muslim world should set you up for life. Instead of wasting your time on cults and political activists, or countless retreats and intensive courses, you will be able to invest your faith in the scholars of old, those sages and luminaries who have stood the test of time. You will have access to their books and to the living teachers who carry their legacy today. This means that nothing will faze you. The "age we live in" argument will never cross your mind, let alone your heart, because what you have access to is timeless. You will be able to focus on studying and learning, growing and developing and, of course, most importantly, enjoying and relishing your faith and your direct relationship with your Lord.

---

[77] Please see this biography of Imam Ismāʿīl ibn Badrān for further details: http://meeraath.infofiend.org/?page_id=144 (Accessed Dec 6, 2016) One can also see the hundreds of *fatwas*, or legal opinions, that just these two imams left behind, in print and online, answering questions from Muslims all over the world. Imam al-Būṭī, in the last four to five years of his life, gave almost 600 fatwas, which were recently published as book by the naseemalsham website. The same cannot be said of any "scholar" in the Anglosphere.
[78] Please see the article for further details: http://mahdinnm.blogspot.com/2016/02/authority-in-islam.html (Accessed Dec 6, 2016) as well as https://mahdinnm.blogspot.com/2016/10/religion-of-peace.html (Accessed July 13, 2018)

Chapter 5: Getting Over Your Childhood: You are not a new Muslim forever

"If you tried to number Allah's blessings, you could never count them." [an-Naḥl 16:18]

The greatest compliment I ever receive is when someone tells me that they had no idea I was a convert. They thought my parents were Muslims and that I was raised in a Muslim household. This means a lot to me because it means that Islam, while obviously being special to me, has become normal for me. It is now part of who I am. I have become secure and settled in my faith. I am not insecure and unsettled.

A lingering doubt that hangs over converts, as was indicated above when I mentioned convert recidivism, is that they might leave Islam one day. Muslims who were born and raised in Muslim families wonder how committed converts are, or they question their motives for embracing Islam.

In the first chapter, I heavily stressed the importance of conviction, but this applies to both converts and all other Muslims. We are all duty bound to ask ourselves: why am I a Muslim? Am I only a Muslim because my parents are Muslims? If my parents were Hindus, would I just be a Hindu? Am I only a Muslim because at the time I had that crisis, I happened to know some Muslims? If I had happened to know some Mormons, would I have just become a Mormon and still be one today?

This type of introspection is absolutely necessary. For converts, i.e. people who have made a conscious, voluntary decision to become Muslims, the introspection has to be a bit deeper. Why did we make this decision? A few examples of motives have been mentioned above, such as social needs, or the need for discipline in one's life, or a crisis such as a drug problem, divorce, death of a loved one etc.

In this chapter, I would like to look at another factor, which is your childhood. What kind of home did you grow up in? Was it stable and healthy or was it abusive? What kind of relationship do you have with your parents and siblings? Are they healthy individuals or are they abusive and toxic? Were you subjected to physical, verbal, or emotional abuse, or worse? Are you still?

If all or any of the above are true, depending on the nature of the abuse, you may need to seek professional help, which I am not qualified to give. Rather, I would like to focus on how your childhood experience may a) affect your decision to become Muslim and b) affect your spiritual growth and development thereafter.

As indicated in the article cited above about ginger converts, Islam must not be used as a vehicle or outlet for one's pent-up frustration and rage against one's society or the world at large. This is how extremism comes about. If you feel that throughout your life people have always bullied you, mocked you, ridiculed you, needlessly criticised you and put you down, do not become a Muslim so that you can get back at these people, individually or in general. If this is your intent, consciously or subconsciously, you will eat yourself alive in the long run.

Instead, you need to reframe the bullying and the abuse. You need to look at it differently. It is not your fault that you were bullied, but you have to ask: why have so many people felt that they could bully you and get away with it? What weakness could they detect from you, and why is it there?

This is why I take it back to your childhood and to your parents and possibly your siblings as well. If you were mercilessly mocked and ridiculed by members of your own family, and especially one or both of your parents, and then put down further if you tried to defend yourself, it is highly likely that you developed a strong sense of shame.[79] In her excellent book *Toxic Parents*, psychologist Susan Forward talks about how abusive parents inculcate harmful subconscious beliefs into their children, and subconscious beliefs are the beliefs you will always act in accordance with, no matter what.

For example, if members of your family mocked you for an opinion you voiced and then put you down again when you tried to defend yourself, your subconscious belief might be 'I'm stupid. My ideas are stupid. No one will ever take me seriously.' If you were called selfish and arrogant for trying to stick up for yourself,

---

[79] The difference between shame and guilt is that guilt is attached to a deed, i.e. something that you said or did, while shame is attached to you as a person. This is it why it is so much more toxic and destructive: https://www.psychologytoday.com/blog/the-squeaky-wheel/201305/5-reasons-why-some-people-will-never-say-sorry (Accessed Dec 22, 2016)

your subconscious belief might be, 'I am selfish and arrogant. I should never stick up for myself. I am selfish if I try to stick up for myself.' Sometimes, the mockery and abuse can be so bad that your very existence feels shameful, and thus you subconsciously make yourself almost unnoticeable, and this can be through you simply not talking as well as in your posture. In other words, you will feel too ashamed to assert yourself in both your speech and your body language. Inevitably, this will give you the appearance of being a pushover and therefore a target for bullies, but the sense you are being wronged will still be felt on the inside, and hence anger and resentment will grow and burn inside you. On a conscious level, you will keep questioning yourself as to why you never stick up for yourself.

Bullies are weak people, and they are usually created by other bullies. What you have to do is break the cycle and not bully others. Whatever was done to you when you were a child is not your fault, but you are responsible for what you do about it as an adult. When it comes to abusive parents or siblings, and toxic people in general, keep a distance. Confronting them can be very therapeutic, but if they show no signs of change, it is better to keep them at arm's length. Don't cut off family, as that's *ḥarām*, keep lines of communication open, but you have to protect yourself and not put yourself in a situation in which you will be exposed to abuse.[80]

---

[80] Please read this *fatwa*: http://mahdinnm.blogspot.com/2016/11/my-father-oppresses-me-greatly.html (Accessed Dec 7, 2016) A further tip that can be added here is that you should not go out of your way to impress such people. If they failed to appreciate you and love you unconditionally before you

Shame is incredibly debilitating. The fundamental subconscious belief that undergirds shame is that one is unworthy. You feel that you are simply not good enough and therefore you don't deserve anything better. This will affect your spiritual growth, without you even noticing, as you will harbour this subconscious belief that you don't deserve to work hard and thus make real progress with your faith.[81] Instead, you will fall into the trap of playing the victim and blaming everyone else for your failures. Every excuse and complaint will be followed by another excuse and complaint. Sometimes the shame is so strong that even when you're aware of it, you're ashamed of what people will think of you if you take steps to change it, because any step to change the

---

embraced Islam, don't expect that to change or improve *after* you become a Muslim. Working extra hard to impress your family, and especially your parents, will destroy you in the long run. You will actually feel that you are serving two masters, the Lord and them. Rather, make your Lord the priority. Make yourself a better person: be hardworking, be organised, be well-mannered, be a winner in every way you can, and if your parents or other family members fail to appreciate that or fail to be impressed by that, that is their problem, not yours.

[81] In general, you have to understand that your childhood experience is how you were programmed, for want of a better word. The people you grew up with and the environment you were in shaped who you are, such that as an adult how you react to situations is more or less predictable. To break out of this, you need to go back into your childhood and figure out what events or what people made you react to certain situations in certain ways, or inculcated your subconscious beliefs. If you don't do this, your spiritual, emotional and even intellectual growth will be stunted. Years will pass by and you will simply be the same person, year after year. You are either progressing or regressing. Standing still is the same as regressing. Also, don't be bitter about your childhood and ask why Allah made you go through it. Rather, look for Allah's wisdom behind it. Lord willing, it will make you a stronger person and a more empathetic person, and from there you will be able to help countless others.

way you are living your life is an admission that something was wrong.

There are plenty of books, videos and articles about shame and subconscious beliefs, and you should take time out to look into the topic if anything I am saying here sounds familiar. From an Islamic standpoint, and by that I mean in terms of theology as opposed to psychology, we believe that we are worthy of our Creator's love, warts and all. Once we realise that Islam is the truth and we accept it in our hearts, we turn to our Lord without any fear of being rejected or ignored, and He expects the same from us.

What does the Lord want from you? Does He want your good deeds? He created your deeds: **"Allah created both you and what you do?"** [as-Ṣāffāt 37:96] He doesn't want or need your deeds. Does He want your sacrifices? The Lord says, **"Their flesh and blood does not reach Allah, but your *taqwā*[82] does reach Him."** [al-Ḥājj 22:37] The answer again is a clear no, so what does He want?

He wants *you.*

Let that sink in.

The Lord says, **"And if My slaves ask you about Me, I am near. I answer the call of the caller when he calls on Me."** [al-Baqarah 2:186]

---

[82] i.e. your piety and consciousness of Allah

The Lord also says, **"Is there any doubt in Allah, the Originator of the heavens and the earth? He calls you in order to forgive you for your sins and to defer you until a specified time."** [Ibrāhīm 14:10]

Your Lord and Creator wants to have a relationship with You, just the way you are. You are worthy of having a relationship with Him, and He is the one calling you and asking you to call on Him.

He created you, so why would He reject you?

To encourage this relationship, Allah promises and He also threatens, but this does not mean that He desires to punish any of His creation.

"Allah has promised the men and women of the hypocrites and unbelievers the Fire of Hell, remaining in it timelessly, forever." [Tawbah 9:67]

"Allah has promised the men and women of the believers, gardens with rivers flowing under them, remaining in them timelessly, forever." [Tawbah 7:72]

But then He says,

"Those who disbelieved will be addressed, 'Allah's hatred of the fact that you were called to faith and disbelieved is greater than your hatred of yourselves."[83] [Ghāfir 40:10]

---

[83] i.e. on the Day of Judgment, when they will realise that their entire existence has been a waste

Allah hates the fact that people reject faith. He doesn't desire eternal damnation for anyone, but He keeps His promise:

"Allah will not break His promise. [Āl 'Imrān 3:9]

This is the core of humanity's relationship with their Lord and Creator, and based on what has been laid out, once human beings have entered into a relationship, that relationship is based on three motives: fear of punishment, hope for reward and worshipping Allah simply for Who He is. The last motive is obviously the most praiseworthy.

If you are a teacher or if you have ever been a student, you may have noticed that students, especially children, fall into a similar set of three categories. There are those who will only work unless they are threatened with some sort of punishment. Then there are those who will work when incentivised by some sort of reward. However, the best students of all are those who study and work hard simply because they love to learn, or they love the subject.

Shame plays no part in this relationship. Allah wants you to love Him and worship Him for who He is. At the same time, He accepts you for who you are and He does not expect you to be perfect. You will sin. However, you should aim to avoid sin as much as possible and any sinning should be followed by remorse and repentance. In an authentic ḥadīth from Abū Hurayrah, quoted by Imam Muslim in his famous collection, the Messenger of Allah, may Allah bless him and grant him peace, said, {By the One in Whose Hand is my soul, if you did not sin, Allah would get rid of you and bring people who did sin and they would seek Allah the Exalted's forgiveness and He would forgive them.}[84]

Sinning and then seeking forgiveness is part and parcel of your relationship with your Creator. It is not about shame. Rather, you recognise and acknowledge that as a human being you are weak. You should always strive to improve yourself, but don't strive to perfect yourself. Perfection is for Allah alone.

"Allah desires to make things lighter for you. Man was created weak." [al-Nisā' 4:28]

Your relationship with your Lord and Creator should be two steps forward, one step back, always developing but not in a straight line. You will thrive and bask in His glory, but at other times you will falter and slip. Then you will thrive again. Sometimes you will feel closer to the Lord and at other times you will feel distant, and there is benefit in that. You should miss Him. Sometimes a tribulation will afflict you, you will turn to Allah in supplication and ask for help and then it will hit you.

---

[84] Another brilliant example is the 42nd hadīth in Imam an-Nawawī's famous "Forty" collection, on the authority of Anas, may Allah be pleased with him, in which the Messenger of Allah, may Allah bless him and grant him peace, quotes the Lord as saying, {O son of Adam, as long as you call on Me and have hope in Me, I will forgive you for whatever sins you commit, and they are almost nothing to Me. Son of Adam, if your sins were to reach the clouds in the sky and then you sought forgiveness from Me, I would forgive you. Son of Adam, if you were to come to Me with wrong actions that almost fill the earth but then you met Me without having associated partners with Me, I would definitely come to you with the same amount of forgiveness.}

You haven't supplicated to Allah in a long time. You've been missing this and yearning for this but you never realised.

Then you will turn to Allah and supplicate and it might take a while for an answer to come, for you to be relieved of your affliction. Rest assured that your supplication will be answered at the best time. In the meantime, your relationship should actually flourish. Have a good opinion of your Lord.

On the authority of Abū Hurayrah, in a ḥadīth related by Imams al-Bukhārī and Muslim, the Messenger of Allah, may Allah bless him and grant him peace, said,

{Allah the Exalted says, 'I am as My slave thinks of Me. I am with Him when he remembers. If he remembers Me within Himself, I remember Him within myself. If He remembers Me in a gathering, I remember him in a gathering that is superior. If he draws nearer to Me by the span of a hand, I draw nearer to him by the span of an arm. If He draws nearer to Me by the span of an arm, I draw nearer to him by the span of outstretched arms. If he comes to Me walking, I come to him running.}

Allah will never turn His back on you. Humanity can and does do that to Him. The choice is yours. To keep your relationship on track, and to maintain calm and to keep your emotions in check, you have to have a good opinion of Allah, which is obviously harder when times are hard.

An excellent way to keep focused and to have a good opinion of your Lord is to focus on the blessings that you enjoy. Every day, before you go to bed, take a pen and some paper and write down ten things you are grateful for. Yes, writing them out by hand will have a much greater effect than merely typing them or thinking them over in your head. Try to write ten different things every day. Of course, there are things that you are grateful for every day, such as your faith, your family, your health, your house, your job etc., and you might write all these things down on your first day. As time goes on, you will start to notice how Allah does things for you every day. You will thank Him for all the people you know, such as your neighbours, your colleagues, your concierge, your barber, your green grocer, and so on and so forth. Then you will thank Allah for the "little" things. Maybe you were driving home one day and thought you had a popped tire and wanted to get it checked, but you had no idea where to go. Then some roadworks forced you to take a detour from your normal route and presto, there was a tyre shop right in front of you. Lord willing, even in the worst of times, you will see Allah doing things for you every day, over and over again. You will never run out of blessings to count. There are so many all around us and we fail to appreciate them because we don't take the time, just a few minutes, to stop and reflect on them. Lord willing, even if a bad thing or several bad things happen on one day, you will still see every day as a good day.

In connection to this, to keep yourself optimistic and in a good frame of mind, and to avoid shame and anxiety, you have to avoid negative people, or toxic people. Negative people live lives that are the opposite of what is described above. They always talk about what's wrong and keep their focus on what's wrong. Calling these people toxic is thoroughly accurate because being in their presence will poison you. They will make you feel anxious and stressed, and if they don't have an actual bad thing to whinge about, guess what? They'll think of something hypothetical to complain about, something that hasn't even happened yet, but might. You know who these people are in your own life. You need to take protective measures.

Similar people will try to take you down when you attempt to make a big step in your life and fulfill your potential. Everyone has the potential to do great things but not everyone has the courage and dedication. When you do something great for yourself, a lot of people will be envious of you and will attack you because you will be exposing their lack of courage and dedication. Doing something great for yourself would obviously include following your conviction and becoming a Muslim. A lot of people simply do not have that courage. They worry about their families and their careers. They worry about what people are going to think and say about them. For most people, life is a lot easier if you just go along to get along. Why rock the boat? Why ruffle feathers? However, if you can tell yourself, 'I'm not going to Hell for anyone', that will give you courage to overcome these obstacles and deal with whatever criticism may come your way.

Still, avoid toxic people as much as possible. They will take you down to their level and then beat you on experience. Spare yourself the shame and spare yourself the stress and anxiety. Once you've embraced Islam, you have to get used to the fact that people who are not Muslim will not be impressed, to say the least. Do not expect any kind words or favours from them. Interestingly, the Lord says,

"Many of the People of the Book would love it if they could make you revert to being unbelievers after you have become believers, showing their innate envy now that the truth is clear to them." [al-Baqarah 2:109]

If you've become a Muslim based on conviction and you allow that conviction to guide your subsequent decisions, i.e. what kind of Muslim you're going to be, what you're going to study, who you're going to study with, and so forth, a lot of Muslims will not be impressed by you, especially those who have become Muslims for motives other than pure conviction. You will be making them look bad and even worse you will be making them *feel* bad. Feelings are very important in Europe and the Anglosphere in this day and age, far more important than facts and objective standards.[85]

Spiritual and emotional development are connected to physical development. Take care of your health. Eat well and get sufficient exercise. You have to understand that your body is an instrument of worship and it is a trust from Allah. Allah has entrusted it to you so that you can carry out your obligations towards Him and the creation. In terms of economics, we're in the middle between communists and libertarians: it's not the state that owns your body nor is it you. Allah owns it and

---

[85] For daily habits that enhance your spirit, you can try this: http://mahdinnm.blogspot.com/2012/11/a-daily-wird.html (Accessed Dec 9, 2016)

therefore He decides what you can do with it and what you can put inside of it.

There are well-known matters that Allah has declared unlawful, such as pork and alcohol, but we should also note that every time Allah commands believers to eat ḥalāl, i.e. lawful, food in the Qur'ān, He also mentions the word *tayyib*, which means pure and wholesome:

"O mankind! Eat what is lawful and *tayyib* on the earth." [al-Baqarah 2:168]

"Eat the lawful and *tayyib* things that Allah has provided for you." [al-Mā'idah 5:88]

"So make full use of any spoils you have taken which is lawful and *tayyib*. [al-Anfāl 8:69]

"So eat from what Allah has provided for you, lawful and *tayyib*, and be thankful for the blessing of Allah if it is Him you worship." [an-Naḥl 16:114]

Just because something is free from alcohol or pork, it doesn't mean that you can or should necessarily eat it. Most of the "mainstream" food in the Anglosphere, i.e. the food that you find in your local grocery store or supermarket, is processed and manufactured. It doesn't go off for weeks and has several unpronounceable ingredients. You need to research to see what suits your body, but as a general rule, avoid sugar and that which mimics sugar, such as aspartame and high fructose corn syrup. You should also avoid flavour enhancers like monosodium glutamate. As indicated above, if you can't read it, it's better you don't eat it, but please do your own research if you doubt what I am saying.

Also, don't eat to excess. Allah says, **"Children of Adam! Wear fine clothing in every masjid and eat and drink but do not be profligate. He does not love the profligate."** [al-ʾAʿrāf 7:31] The best thing you can read in English on the topic of eating is the article 'Protecting the Stomach' by Imam al-Ghazālī.[86] Being obese does not match a spiritual life as it indicates that you cannot control your desires and cravings. It will also expose your body to disease and decay.

Exercise is also very important. Think of it this way: if you were told that your first car had to last you your entire life, how would you treat it? You only have one body. If it breaks down, you can't replace it with another one. There is no return or refund policy. You don't have to train like a professional athlete, but you should at least do some walking every day. Some people like to go to the gym and lift weights for a couple hours a few days a week. I prefer to do intense floor exercises at home, such as push-ups and cross-body mountain climbers, and by intense I mean something that makes me breathe heavily and sweat profusely. It allows me to release whatever stress or negative energy I have inside me and after a shower I feel a lot sharper and perkier.

You should also take into consideration how you look, and I don't mean that in a vain sense. As Muslims we are ambassadors

---

[86] http://mahdinnm.blogspot.com/2015/06/imam-al-ghazali-on-protecting-stomach.html (Accessed Dec 9, 2016)

for our faith, and especially if we embraced Islam at a later point in life. We need to show that we are winners, that becoming Islam has made us better people. If we were lazy before, now we are industrious. If we were ill-informed before, now we are studious and diligent. If we were obese and lethargic before, now we are fit and active. If we were scruffy and unkempt before, now we are neat and smart.[87] Do not make the horrible assumption that Islam is monasticism[88] and therefore it is praiseworthy to look as if you sleep on the streets. Also, try to cover your head.[89]

---

[87] For further details on this, I highly recommend the book *Islamic Manners* by Sheikh ʿAbdul Fattāḥ Abū Ghuddah.

[88] Allah says, **"They invented monasticism-we did not prescribe it for them."** [al-Ḥadīd 57:27] Furthermore, in the authentic collections of Imam al-Bukhārī and Muslim, there is the ḥadīth on the authority of Anas in which three Companions came to the Prophet's wives, may Allah bless him and grant him peace, and asked about how the Prophet, may Allah bless him and grant him peace, was in private. Afterwards, one of them said, 'I will not marry women.' Another one said, 'I will not eat meat.' Another one said, 'I will not sleep on a bed.' The Messenger of Allah, may Allah bless him and grant him peace, then came and said, {What is with these people who said such and such? I pray and I sleep. I fast and I break my fast, and I marry women. Whoever turns away from my Sunnah is not of me.} [*Ṣaḥīḥ Muslim bi Sharḥ an-Nawawī* (Beirut: Dār al-Kutub al-ʿIlmiyyah, 1424/2003), v.9, p.150] Instead, a believer should make sure he does not identify with material things, regardless of their quality or quantity. Their existence in your possession does not add to who you are and their absence would not diminish who you are.

[89] 'It is recommended for a man to wear his best and most perfect clothes when praying, and there is nothing more perfect than the clothes that he adorns himself with in the company of people, such as that which covers his body, and he wears an *ʿamāmah* [an Islamic way of tying a turban] and upper garment. It has been mentioned from Ibn ʿUmar, may Allah be pleased with him, that he saw his servant Nāfiʿ praying bareheaded, so he said to him, "If you were to go out into the presence of people, do you think you would go out

Being physically fit and having a smart appearance will enhance your confidence, and this will feed into your emotional and spiritual health. It will also protect you from any sense of shame. You don't just want to be a Muslim, you want to thrive. Being on the winning team is nice, but it will never satisfy you as much as being a winner in this life as well as the next. Respect yourself, push yourself, and set high standards for yourself. Never expect life to get easier. Rather, work hard and expect it to get better.

Another serious challenge you're going to face, and this is the second half of this chapter, is getting over the "convert", "revert" or "new Muslim" label.

First of all, "revert" is an utterly ridiculous and idiotic term. To revert means to return to a former habit, practice, belief, condition etc. Yes, every child is born on *al-fiṭrah*, i.e. the natural disposition of human beings, and Islam is the religion of *al-fiṭrah*, it is the religion that accurately corresponds to man's natural disposition. The argument thus goes that by embracing Islam

---

like this?" He replied, "No". He said, "Then Allah is more deserving of being adorned for." This has been related by Abū Dāwūd and others.

It is recommended for a woman to pray in three garments: a *khimār* that covers her head and neck, a chemise (*dirʿ*) that covers her body and feet and thick *milḥafah*–and a *milḥafah* is a jilbāb–due to what has been related from ʿUmar, may Allah be pleased with him, in which he said, "A woman prays in three garments: a chemise, a *khimār* and a lower garment (*izār*)." It is also on the authority of ʿAbdullah ibn ʿUmar, may Allah be pleased with both of them, who said, "A woman prays in a chemise, a *khimār* and a *milḥafah*." Imam ash-Shāfiʿī said, "People in general have agreed on the chemise and the *khimār*, and whatever is added to that is better and more concealing."' [*Ghāyat al-Munā* by Sheikh Muḥammad Bā ʿAṭiyyah (Amman: Dār al-Fatḥ, n.d), p.271]

one returns to one's natural disposition. Great. But who made the decision to leave in the first place? I never made the decision not to be Muslim or the decision to move away from my natural disposition. I never apostated. To me, this was a discovery, not a homecoming. A synonym of to revert is to retrogress, i.e. to go backward into an earlier and usually worse condition. Becoming a Muslim is supposed to be progress; I'm supposed to be gradually moving towards a better condition. I loathe this term and would prefer for it not to be used.

The term "new Muslim" is a temporary term. You can't be a "new" Muslim for more than a year. Once you're in the habit of praying five times a day, and you know enough basic Arabic to do so, and you've fasted an entire Ramadan, you should really stop referring to yourself as a "new" Muslim, and you should prevent others from doing so as well. You have to move on and start taking responsibility. How long are you considered a "new" employee when you start work somewhere? How long are you considered "new in town" when you move somewhere? Think about that. You do not want to fall into the trap of having a victim mentality and thus use the excuse of being a "new" Muslim for years and years when people ask you why you still haven't learned the basics of your faith, or haven't made much progress in general. This is a pathetic attitude to have.

"Convert" is an accurate term because it is a permanent truth. Instead of being raised by Muslim parents in a Muslim household, a convert has made the conscious decision to become a Muslim, and usually against the wishes and advice of his parents, family, culture, society and so forth. However, the usefulness of the term "convert" is just that, i.e. to distinguish you from those who were born and raised in Muslim households. Aside from that, the term "convert" is useless and we really should just talk about Muslims, regardless of how they got there. There are a few reasons.

For starters, not everyone who is raised in a "Muslim" household receives an "Islamic" upbringing. That's why we have these funny terms in English like "practicing Muslim", as if it's a hobby like ballet or a branch of medicine. A child in this situation may be told that he is a Muslim, or that his family is Muslim, but that doesn't mean that people in his family will pray, fast, go the masjid and so forth. A person in this situation faces three possibilities:

1. Follow the family and be a "secular Muslim", i.e. Muslim in name only. You could also say "cultural" Muslim.
2. Realise that being a "secular Muslim" is not only contradictory but a complete waste of time, and thus he formally leaves Islam and no longer calls himself a Muslim.
3. Try to discover Islam outside of his family and local community.

The last one branches out into lots of further possibilities, because in such a case this person is not very different from a convert. They've made the conscious decision to be a Muslim, their family is most likely not supportive and therefore they have to go elsewhere. They could fall in with cultists and political activists, they could get swept away by a Sufi brotherhood, they might be enticed by the hippie converts and their affiliates, or they might come across some sincere believers and get the opportunity to study Arabic along with basic theology and *fiqh*.

As a side note, the last option is not likely in the Anglosphere, and that's why I think "secular Muslims" should be honest and just leave the faith. Don't raise children and tell them they're Muslims but then never explain it to them or even demonstrate it to them. This will just make them easy prey for the various organisations that I've mentioned above.[90] They will feel horribly confused as they won't know what to make of their parents. They might have thoughts like: "My dad says he's a Muslim but he drinks alcohol", "My mom says she's a Muslim but she never prays." With Islam, do it or don't do it. Doing it doesn't mean being perfect in all of one's actions. Rather, it means being fully committed in the general sense. You may slip here and there or not feel ready to commit to *certain* things, but as long as you recognise and acknowledge that you have progress to make and that you're working on it, you'll be fine. The problem with "cultural" Muslims is the sense of satisfaction. They are lukewarm Muslims, in that they pick and choose what they want to "practise", they are happy the way they are and, to make matters worse, they expect their children to follow their lead. If you claim to follow a religion, or a legal system or a constitution, and then you blatantly only follow that which suits your desires and interests, this is clear hypocrisy and your children will notice it.

---

[90] This is a typical example: http://www.dailymail.co.uk/news/article-3457741/Heartbroken-hopeless-Parents-Scottish-jihadi-bride-Aqsa-Mahmood-tell-devastation-losing-ISIS-brainwashing.html (Accessed Dec 10, 2016)

It's much better to be honest and to admit that you are not a Muslim, or that you follow whatever *you* think is best.

Therefore, based on the aforementioned, if you're a convert, don't let any so-called "born Muslim" assert his authority over you. His Muslim name or the fact that he was raised in a Muslim household is no indicator of authority, but a conversation like this is typical:

'Ma sha Allah, brother, how long have you been Muslim?'

'Three years.'

"Ma sha Allah, brother, that is great. I have been Muslim for 30 years. I need to explain something to you...'

This is a preposterous argument. 30 years, or whatever figure someone gives you, is their age. It doesn't mean anything. When a convert says 'I've been a Muslim for X years', it means that they have been conscious, willing Muslims for that period of time. A "born Muslim" thinks that simply being alive means the same thing, or at least he wants *you* to think that. Don't fall for it. Instead, ask this individual how long he has been a committed believer. Ask him what he has studied, and whom with. It's very likely that this "born Muslim" has been a committed believer for about as long as you have, maybe less.

Furthermore, if you converted to Islam in your teenage years, and there are plenty of people who embrace Islam in early adolescence, unless a "born Muslim" is from a scholarly family and grew up reading and memorising texts and studying with his parents, there is no way such a person can claim that being a Muslim longer than you have means anything, let alone scholarly authority over you.

Of course, as a convert, people will want to ask you how and why you became Muslim, and that's fair enough, especially "born Muslims" who have been raised in more "cultural" or secular families. They want to understand how and why someone would choose Islam completely voluntarily, without any pressure from their family, community or broader culture. Your story may very well be inspiring and even include aspects that are beyond material explanation. Share your story and inspire people, absolutely, but don't let your story define who you are.

Please let me explain what I mean by that. About six years ago I was invited to speak at a masjid in the United Kingdom about Ramadan and how to prepare for the end of Ramadan. My talk was brief and on point and I basically gave spiritual advice about how to make the benefits of Ramadan carry on throughout the rest of the year. After that, the floor was opened for questions. The majority of the congregation were Pakistanis, i.e. "born Muslims", and the vast majority of questions I received, over a period of about half an hour, was about how I became Muslim and not the topic at hand.

In a situation like this, I keep my answers brief. The event had nothing to do with converting to Islam and therefore anything more than a brief answer would be a digression from the topic. Furthermore, I do not want to encourage this type of questioning should I ever speak at the same masjid or anywhere else. If I encourage it, I would allow my conversion story and the fact that I'm a convert subsume my identity, which would be perilous. Yes, I converted, but it was a very long time ago and I have since moved on with my life. I don't want special treatment. Every Companion of the Messenger of Allah, may Allah bless him and grant him peace, was a convert, and most of them in adulthood. They learned the faith, they applied it and they moved on.

Some "born Muslims", especially those who have only been around Muslims of their own ethnicity, or have a general assumption that only Arabs or Asians can be Muslim, will have a hard time believing that you are actually a Muslim. They'll have an even harder time believing that you've actually learned anything about Islam. The fact that you pray five times a day and know what to say in your prayer might actually shock them. May Allah have mercy on these people. You may find them to be incredibly patronising and condescending, but it's best to smile and keep a safe distance. If they annoy you by constantly gawking at you or asking you silly questions, try to get someone of the same ethnic group or nationality to have a polite word with them. Either way, people like this are not worth stressing over.

Then there are other "born Muslims" who will assume that converts are blank slates that have no past worth mentioning or remembering. There are three ways of looking at this.

First of all, there is the assumption that converts don't have any negative baggage, i.e. cultural baggage that contradicts Islam in any way. "Born Muslims" obviously grow up in households that have a certain culture, whether that culture is Pakistani,

Moroccan, Iraqi, Malaysian, whatever, and that culture will at times (some cultures more than others) contradict the faith. "Born Muslims" are under constant pressure from their families and communities to comply with their culture, and in some cases the culture is so diametrically opposed to the faith, because it includes forced marriage, honour killings, acid throwing, child rape etc., that someone born into the culture has to strive and struggle to their utmost to escape from it. If the culture doesn't reach such a horrific level, there will still be arguments and battles when it comes to the implementation of the faith. Converts, having defied or at least surprised their families, do not have *these* particular issues.

Secondly, not having the cultural issues above does not mean that converts should completely ignore or discard whatever culture they grew up in. They only have to discard that which contradicts the faith. So, if you're English, four o'clock tea is perfectly fine. A pint at the pub is not. Being generally reserved and minding one's own business is fantastic. Reading tabloid newspapers and gossip magazines, which are full of rumours and fluff that are of no concern to you, is not. Being organised and orderly (including knowing how to stand in a queue), as well as being punctual and neat, is absolutely praiseworthy. Being a gentleman and respecting women, regardless of race or religion, is absolutely praiseworthy. Not being hypersensitive and reacting swiftly to any perceived offense is absolutely praiseworthy. Do not completely discard the culture you grew up in. Take what is good and praiseworthy about it and leave what isn't, and then do the same with whatever culture "born Muslims" present to you. Don't let "born Muslims" impose their culture on you on the grounds that their ethnic group or nationality is Muslim and yours isn't. Again, the key here is knowledge, not the mere fact that someone or a group of people are Muslims.

Thirdly, as indicated earlier in this chapter, converts can and do have psychological baggage. Their conversion to Islam might be primarily motivated by some emotional or psychological need, and if that need is not met they may very well move on to something else. If they remain within Islam, it is highly likely that they will move from one group or organisation to another, especially if they are looking for a leader or leadership structure to look after them. As Eric Hoffer states in his book *The True Believer*, the real motive here is the fear of an autonomous existence. The doctrines of the group or organisation are irrelevant.

Again, we're back at the importance of conviction.

Chapter 6: Culture and Media

"The Jews and the Christians will never be pleased with you until you follow their religion." [al-Baqarah 2:120]

"You will be tested in your wealth and in yourselves and you will hear much harm from those given the Book before you and from those who are idolaters. But if you are steadfast and are godfearing, that is the most resolute course to take." [Āl 'Imrān 3:186]

"That is because they hate what Allah has sent down…" [Muḥammad 47:7]

In the previous chapter, I mentioned the importance of avoiding toxic people for the sake of one's emotional and spiritual health, but toxicity is not only liable to be found in the people you know or meet in person. Rather, it can permeate a culture and be especially prevalent in the media.

At the time of writing this chapter, the so called mainstream media in the Anglosphere is in absolute meltdown. In the past year, media organisations like the BBC, CNN, *The New York Times*, *The Guardian*, and *The Washington Post* have witnessed massive setbacks to their supposed control of the narrative. Their promotion of the European Union and labelling of all "Eurosceptics" as racists and xenophobes failed to prevent the British people from voting to leave the EU project. 17.4 million people voted to leave, the largest electoral mandate in British history. Then, a few months later, Donald J. Trump beat Hillary Clinton in the 2016 US presidential election. The mainstream

94

media did everything to portray Trump as a racist, sexist, bigot, xenophobe, Nazi, you name it, and, to top it off, they said he had no chance of winning. He won in an electoral landslide.[91]

What this means is that these "mainstream" organisations lost control of the narrative. The people who voted to leave the EU or voted for Donald Trump turned to the internet and to alternative media for their news and for information about the EU and both US presidential candidates, as well as social media. In the case of the EU referendum, there was the Breitbart London website, as well as the Twitter pages and YouTube videos of people like Daniel Hannan[92] and Nigel Farage. In the case of the 2016 US Elections, Trump himself used his Twitter page with deft skill and proficiency, as well as Facebook, to simply bypass the "mainstream" media and get his message out to millions of voters.[93] On top of that, there were the YouTube videos of people

---

[91] Some people will most likely object here and say that Hillary Clinton won the popular vote. There is no popular vote in the United States as a whole. Rather, each state has its own election and each county within each state has its own election. Trump won the vast majority of counties and states, and therefore he represents a far wider spectrum of American voters. Furthermore, if the federal election were based on a popular vote, Trump would have campaigned differently and voters would have behaved differently. For example, there are plenty of Republicans in predominantly liberal states like California and New York but they don't bother to vote because they know that their state is going to be won by the Democrats.
[92] Hannan's book *Why Vote Leave* is the seminal book on the topic and is a must-read if one wants to fully understand why so many people voted to leave. Sovereignty and economics are far more important to people than immigration.
[93] At the same time, he played the mainstream media to his advantage, knowing that they needed him for their ratings far more than he needed them for publicity. In the end, his campaign only spent half as much money as

like Stefan Molyneux in Canada and Paul Joseph Watson in the United Kingdom, whose video on Hillary Clinton's health now has over 5.5 million views,[94] as well as his Twitter account and that of Mike Cernovich,[95] whose Periscopes also played a huge role. This was in addition to immensely popular websites like Infowars and Breitbart. The latter reached 45 million regular readers after the election.[96]

After the 2016 election, the corporate media organisations started pushing the narrative that Russia influenced the election, without a shred of evidence. They did not want to accept the fact that Trump beat Clinton based on policy and what he represents. Rather, it had to be because the Russian government pushed propaganda that brainwashed so many Americans into voting for him. Yes, this is what they are more or less suggesting.

Anglosphere Muslims have a very interesting relationship with the "mainstream", or corporate, media. When it comes to reporting on Islam and Muslims, the general consensus amongst Muslims in the Anglosphere is that the media is not to be trusted. They distort. They exaggerate. They take words out of context.

Hillary Clinton's campaign: http://www.washingtontimes.com/news/2016/dec/10/hillary-clinton-breaks-president-obamas-2012-spend/ (Accessed Dec 13, 2016)

[94] https://www.youtube.com/watch?v=OqbDBRWb63s (Accessed Dec 12, 2016)

[95] Cernovich is the author of *Gorilla Mindset*, which is an immensely beneficial book for learning how to control your emotions and be positive and optimistic, but to understand culture and why Trump won, *MAGA Mindset*, which was published just a few weeks before the election, cannot be recommended highly enough.

[96] http://www.breitbart.com/big-journalism/2016/11/19/breitbart-news-hits-300-million-pageviews-45-million-uniques-last-31-days/ (Accessed Sept 26, 2017)

They portray Muslims as extremists and terrorists. They only focus on bad news about Muslims, and so on and so forth. However, when those same media organisations report on something else, such as the European Union, or climate change, or people like Donald Trump, Nigel Farage, Tommy Robinson, and so forth, they are believed unflinchingly and wholeheartedly. This is cognitive dissonance at best, hypocrisy at worst.

Allah says, **"You who believe! If a *fāsiq* brings you a report, scrutinise it carefully in case you attack people in ignorance and so come to greatly regret what you have done."** [al-Ḥujurāt 49:6]

A *fāsiq* is someone who is not to be trusted. They have a reputation for dishonesty. If certain media organisations are known for lying, distorting and exaggerating when it comes to Islam and Muslims, why should they be trusted with any other issue?

I have had personal run-ins with the corporate media, including the BBC and *The New York Times*, and I have seen first-hand how they distort and omit. It is indeed frustrating, but one has to step back and realise that there is always an agenda at play. Corporate media organisations have owners and owners have agendas. Sometime the agenda is simply to make a profit, and sometimes the agenda is more sinister, such as some form of social or cultural engineering.[97] TV news, in particular, is primarily about

---

[97] For example, *The New York Times* runs at a loss but is largely-owned by Mexican billionaire Carlos Slim. He's not exactly making money from his investment but he has a major platform with which to influence public

advertising. This means that a television news broadcast has to attract viewers and those viewers in turn will watch the advertisements. In order to attract viewers, that news has to be, well, attractive. It has to entertain. It has to draw attention. Therefore, it has to be sensational. The best book on this topic is *How to Watch TV News* by Neil Postman and Steve Powers.[98] Having a TV in your house because you want to keep up with current events and be "informed" is not an excuse. TV news, at best, is about grabbing your attention and holding on to it long enough so that you watch the commercials.

However, we no longer live in a world in which we are dependent on television and newspapers for our news. The Internet, followed by the advent of social media, has changed all of that. We now have so-called citizen journalists, which means people who report on events and publicise them on their own platforms, such as a website, blog, YouTube video or on social media networks like Twitter, Facebook, Gab etc. I have given examples above of people who do this successfully. This means that in the case of an election campaign, if one wants to know something about a candidate, from their political positions to their life story, one does not have to rely on second-hand information from

opinion. See: http://www.reuters.com/article/us-new-york-times-warrants-carlos-slim-idUSKBN0KN2M820150114 (Accessed Dec 13, 2016). The article also mentions Jeff Bezos, the founder of Amazon, who now owns *The Washington Post*.

[98] I wrote a review several years ago: http://mahdinnm.blogspot.com/2011/03/utter-waste-of-time-and-money.html (Accessed Dec 13, 2016) For the evils of television in general, please read Postman's *Amusing Ourselves to Death*.

some reporter at a newspaper or major news network. Rather, one can visit the candidate's own website or social media pages. When news broke of Donald Trump's statement on Muslim immigration to the United States, I immediately went to his personal website to read the statement in full.[99] I didn't waste my time reading it through the filter of the BBC or whoever else.

In the Anglosphere, Muslims, and especially their self-anointed leaders, are struggling to move beyond reliance on the corporate media, and the recent US election has made this abundantly clear. Muslim leadership, including the hippie converts, fell for the mainstream media narrative about Donald Trump hook, line and sinker. They believed he was a racist and raging Islamophobe, and to make matters worse, they believed that he would never win. Now, after his victory, they are in a state of utter shock. Despite being lead down the garden path by organisations like CNN, Muslims in America went back to them afterwards and poured their hearts out.[100] Muslims in America, like other minorities in the Anglosphere, believed that the leftist candidate would be better for them. Why is that?

The answer to that is cultural and political, and includes the subject of why Muslims are even in the Anglosphere.

---

[99] And I wrote about it here, with a link to his website:
http://mahdinnm.blogspot.com/2015/12/why-do-they-support-trump.html
(Accessed Dec 13, 2016)
[100] Have a look at this article as an example:
http://edition.cnn.com/2016/11/09/politics/muslims-trump-reaction/index.html
(Accessed Dec 13, 2016)

The Culture War

The cultural war in the Anglosphere and Europe is between the right and the left, the conservatives and the progressive liberals.[101] In economic terms, the conservatives favour small government and lower taxation.[102] In other words, the role of government is limited to a certain set of responsibilities, such as protecting the borders as resolving disputes. As economist Thomas Sowell explains, conservatives hold to the Thucydidean tragic view of man. Man is inherently flawed and therefore whatever political or economic system he devises and establishes will also be flawed.[103] Life will always be flawed, it will never be perfect. Rather, it is all about trade-offs,[104] and therefore, we just have to learn to tolerate certain things. The best we can hope for is the best set of trade-offs. Perfection is for the next life. Progressive liberals, on the other hand, favour a larger government because they believe that the government, ultimately, can create a better world, if not a perfect one. They are eternal optimists. If the right laws and regulations are passed, eventually perfection will be attained. In other words, the problems of the world are not because man is inherently flawed but because the institutions that govern him are flawed. If the institutions can be perfected then life can be perfected. The extreme right is the belief that there should be no state and thus

---

[101] i.e. not classic liberals
[102] Obviously, a larger government requires higher taxation.
[103] For a short summary, please see this short interview with Thomas Sowell: https://www.youtube.com/watch?v=5KHdhrNhh88 (Accessed Dec 13, 2016)
[104] For example, some people are happier with a lower wage if it means more free time. Other people are happy to work longer hours for a higher wage.

no public sector whatsoever. The extreme left is complete state control and therefore no private sector, or maybe some semblance of a private sector but under complete government control. Examples of this can be found in the Soviet Union or Nazi Germany.

The above is a polite description, but in the video linked above Prof Sowell indicates that there is something more at play. We have to ask: what kind of people are attracted to the left and what kind of people are attracted to the right?[105] And before that, there's another question: what kind of people become politicians?

As Albert J. Nock described in his book *Our Enemy, The State*, there are two types of people: producers and parasites. There are those who produce what their fellow men need and want, and they exchange it for what they need and want, and then there are those who merely feed off of what the producers produce. Those who have a skill or talent to produce will get a job or start a business, or a combination of both, and move on with their lives. Those who have nothing to offer, i.e. they cannot produce any good or service that anyone would voluntarily pay for, have to find some way to make a living. Humble people will work hard to acquire a marketable talent or skill, and they will work a simple job until they've acquired it, such as washing dishes or cleaning toilets. They won't be a financial burden on anyone. The not so

---

[105] This recent article is also relevant:
http://mahdinnm.blogspot.com/2017/01/why-are-leftists-so-violent-and.html
(Accessed March 13, 2017)

humble will see cleaning toilets as beneath them, and that the reason they're not employed is that few people recognise how special and creative they are, or how deeply they think, and therefore they apply for a job in the government. In the government, you get paid from money that has been taken from people involuntarily, i.e. taxes, to do a job that those people most likely did not ask you to do.[106] The job they seek will most likely involve regulating the lives of those who produce. As Ludwig von Mises puts it in his book *Bureaucracy*, 'He who is unfit to serve his fellow citizens wants to rule them.'[107]

A bureaucratic government job as some sort of regulator or lawmaker suits these narcissists perfectly. It gives them a position from which they can a) satisfy their need to feel important and special and b) vent their jealousy towards the productive class of people by making their lives more and more difficult. This is why democracies always become more and more tyrannical over time. Those who have marketable skills and talents will take those skills and talents to the market. Working in government is below their skillset and their ambitions. They will only run in elections or work in government if they feel there is a genuine need or they simply get fed up of the way bureaucrats and politicians run

---

[106] Please see Martin Durkin's documentary *Britain's Trillion Pound Horror Story* for an excellent illustration of what a great number of government employees do. If they never went to work, no one would notice. Obviously, in this paragraph, I'm not talking about people who do have skills (e.g. doctors, nurses, teachers, firemen etc.) but work for the government, as these people do service genuine needs. Rather, I'm rather to people who have jobs merely for the sake of having jobs, with funky titles like "community cohesion officer" and the like. If these people didn't show up to work, no one would notice.
[107] (New Haven: Yale University Press, 1994) p.92

things. This is what is happening now in the United States. For leftists, a job in the government is their greatest ambition. For those on the right, such a job is only sought out of necessity.

Leftists also receive government salaries in academia, namely in state universities, which is a platform for them to influence public opinion and especially that of youngsters. If they get tenured, it's a job for life, regardless of how many research papers they publish or how many doctoral theses they supervise. Again, we have to ask: to what extent are they providing a good or service that people would voluntarily pay for? For more on this topic, Thomas Sowell's book *Intellectuals and Society* is second to none. Sowell points out that intellectuals, as opposed to doctors or engineers, for example, do not have to suffer their consequences of their bad ideas, even if they lead to the deaths of millions of people. If a doctor makes a mistake and a patient dies, that doctor will suffer. If an engineer makes a mistake and a bridge collapses, that engineer will suffer. Because the main "product" of intellectuals is ideas, the consequences of those ideas are not directly attributable. If the idea or ideology does lead to disastrous consequences, the intellectual who came up with the idea can claim that he had a good intention, or that his idea was not implemented properly, or that the wrong people were in charge.

Seeing as we're talking about the left and the right, let's look at the example of Karl Marx. This is an intellectual who never worked a day in his life yet claimed to be a champion of the working class. He predicted that capitalism would fail and that the workers of the world would rise up. His ideology led to the rise and rule of monsters like Joseph Stalin, Mao Zedong, Fidel Castro, Pol Pot the Kim family of North Korea, and so on and so forth. Millions upon millions have died under the persecution and man-made famines of communist regimes,[108] 94 million between 1900 and 2000, and yet many people in the west still think that communism in their own country would be a good idea.[109] Everywhere it has been implemented that result has been a dictatorship followed by persecution, destruction and death, but there are still those who want to give Karl Marx the benefit of the doubt. He meant well. Communism has never been implemented properly. The wrong people were in charge. As economist Milton Freidman put it, we don't want a system that depends on the right people being in charge. We want a system that forces the wrong people to do the right thing.[110]

For Muslims living in the Anglosphere, we have to understand why Muslims tend to be more aligned with the left than with the right. People on the left want to feel important and needed, and therefore they come across as caring, motherly figures. They

---

[108] https://infogalactic.com/info/Mass_killings_under_Communist_regimes (Accessed Dec 14, 2016)
[109] http://reason.com/blog/2013/03/13/communism-killed-94m-in-20th-century (Accessed Dec 14, 2016)
[110] Or as Daniel Hannan puts it, you can't legislate against greed. Instead, you remove any incentive that would encourage someone to be greedy. Incentives are what truly matters. To assume that a public sector employee is engaged in "public service" while a private sector employee is only looking out for himself is to assume complete and utter nonsense. Both of them are looking out for their own selfish interests, because that's what all human beings, with few exceptions, look out for, but to meet their own selfish needs and interests they have to fulfill the needs and interests of others, and thus we have voluntary exchange and trade.

project an image of caring about minorities: blacks, Hispanics, Muslims, Jews, homosexuals, transgenders etc. Conservatives are portrayed as being cruel, heartless and uncaring.

This sounds a lot like the difference between a mother and a father. A mother is full of mercy and cannot bear the thought of her child experiencing any sort of difficulty or inconvenience. A father is strict and wants his children to be tough, resilient, self-reliant and independent. A healthy child needs both parents, but a child who receives nothing but mercy and never any strictness will suffer in this world. For example, a father might tell his 18-year-old son as he heads off to university, "I've done enough for you. Work hard and make something of yourself. You can come back here to visit but not to live." His mother would shudder at such words, because they do indeed sound harsh, but they will motivate that son to work his socks off and become something. His mother might say, "It's OK. If things don't work out, you can always come home. Don't worry about anything." This sounds sweet and caring, but it's not motivating. The message embedded in these words is that it's OK to fail.

The difference in understanding between the mother and the father is that the former sees her child as a child, and that child needs to be looked after and taken care of. The father sees the child as a child for the time being; eventually all children have to become adults.

With that in mind, look at how the left and the right view poor people. The left seems them as a permanent underclass, a group of people who are always within the lowest income bracket and never come out of it, and therefore they need constant government assistance. The right sees "the poor" as a statistical category; flesh-and-blood human beings move in and out of income brackets throughout the course of their lives and in a healthy economy that trajectory should be upwards. When someone first steps on the job ladder, it is normal for them to be in a lower income bracket, but as they gain experience, and in many cases qualifications, they move into higher income brackets.

The debate over minimum wage legislation is a classic example. The left argues that the poor will be helped by having higher wages. It is not fair to expect someone to live their lives working for such a paltry wage. The right's response is that someone working a low-income job is not expected to work there forever. Rather, that low-income job is merely a stepping stone towards bigger and better things. As economist Walter Williams explains in his documentary *Good Intentions*,[111] as well as Thomas Sowell in numerous writings and interviews,[112] the minimum wage law in the United States has completely decimated black teenage employment. Teenagers don't have any experience or qualifications, so if their productivity and skill don't merit the minimum wage, they don't get hired. Furthermore, teenagers are still living at home with their parents, so rent and bills are not an issue, which means that the wage is not that important. Rather, a

---

[111] http://mahdinnm.blogspot.com/2011/09/good-intentions.html (Accessed Dec 14, 2016)
[112] For example: http://www.nationalreview.com/article/415569/ruinous-compassion-minimum-wage-laws-thomas-sowell (Accessed Dec 14, 2016)

job for a teenager is about gaining skills and experience, about getting on the employment ladder and then working up from there. The minimum wage law effectively removes the bottom rungs of that ladder.

Freedom is inexorably tied to independence. The more independent you are; the more freedom you have. Just as your dependence on your parents as a child limited your options and choices, your dependence on government does the same. When leftists praise communist dictatorships like Castro's Cuba, they always mention the free stuff, such as education and healthcare.[113] When you lived with your parents as a child, you also got loads of free stuff: food, board, clothing, education, healthcare, and so forth, but would you voluntarily give up your adulthood now and go back to that, agreeing to live the rest of your life according to your parents' rules?

This is the trick of the left. While some of them undoubtedly care, and do so sincerely, with age they should come to know better. Their policies ultimately infantilise people and make them dependent on the state. As the saying goes, if you're not a radical in your twenties, you have no heart. If you're still a radical in your forties, you have no head. Those who cling fervently to leftist polices as even they grow older are either lacking in intelligence or there is something wrong psychologically, i.e. such people are narcissists and have a strong psychological desire

---

[113] http://www.commonwealthfund.org/publications/blog/2016/nov/fidel-castros-health-care-legacy (Accessed Dec 14, 2016)

to be needed and to feel important. Thomas Sowell calls such people "the anointed", and he describes them as follows:

'The anointed want to eliminate stress, challenge, striving, and competition. They want the necessities of life to be supplied as "rights" -- which is to say, at the taxpayers' expense, without anyone's being forced to work for those necessities, except of course the taxpayers.

Nothing is to be earned. "Self-esteem" is to be dispensed to the children as largess from the teacher. Adults are to have their medical care and other necessities dispensed as largess from the government. People are to be mixed and matched by race and sex and whatever else the anointed want to take into account, in order to present whatever kind of picture the anointed think should be presented.

This is a vision of human beings as livestock to be fed by the government and herded and tended by the anointed. All the things that make us human beings are to be removed from our lives and we are to live as denatured creatures controlled and directed by our betters.

Those things that help human beings be independent and self-reliant -- whether automobiles, guns, the free market, or vouchers -- provoke instant hostility from the anointed.

Automobiles enable you to come and go as you wish, without so much as a "by your leave" to your betters. The very idea that other people will go where they want, live where they want, how they want, and send their children to whatever schools they choose, is galling to the anointed, for it denies the very specialness that is at the heart of their picture of themselves.

Guns are completely inappropriate for the kind of sheep-like people the anointed envision or the orderly, pre-packaged world in which they are to live. When you are in mortal danger, you are supposed to dial 911, so that the police can arrive on the scene some time later, identify your body, and file reports in triplicate.

The free market is a daily assault on the vision of the anointed. Just think of all those millions of people out there buying whatever they want, whenever they want, whether or not the anointed think it is good for them.

Think of those people earning whatever incomes they happen to get from producing goods or services for other people, at prices resulting from supply and demand, with the anointed cut out of the loop entirely and standing on the sidelines in helpless rage, unable to impose their particular vision of "social justice".

The welfare state is not really about the welfare of the masses. It is about the egos of the elites.'[114]

This mindset is no different from that of a mother who suffers from narcissistic personality disorder. Leftists have an insatiable desire to be needed and relied upon. They hate to see people being independent and free, because it makes them irrelevant and unimportant.

In *How to Watch TV News*, Postman and Powers also point out that the people who present the news on television are there

---

[114] http://townhall.com/columnists/thomassowell/2003/04/21/human_livestock (Accessed Dec 14, 2016)

because they are good anchors and not necessarily because they are good journalists. They look good, and with the help of make-up, a stage, sound effects and other props, they are able to look and sound authoritative. In reality, they are empty shells who simply read off of teleprompters and report what they're told to. Again, we have a class of people who are very similar to career politicians and state-funded academics and intellectuals; people who have no good or service to offer that people would voluntarily pay for. We have another class of talentless, unintelligent narcissists, which means another class of people that are drawn to the left, as it feeds their desire to be in control and to feel important.

This phenomenon was explained by Roosh V in an article he wrote in the summer of 2016:

'When you're at the very top, you sponsor individuals mainly for their ability to advance a particular cause or objective. There's no need for them to be the smartest guy in the room. In fact, being *too* intelligent will actually prevent their hiring because then they will be able to see that their boss doesn't care about "race equality" but fostering race inequality. He doesn't care about "love not hate" but destroying the family unit. Therefore, to work for the elite, you must have huge blind spots that prevent you from seeing the big picture, or at least be sociopathic enough that you are willing to work for an immoral agenda so that you can get closer to the seats of power.

All the people I mentioned earlier, the journalists, politicians, professors, and think tank insiders, were hired primarily for their *usefulness* in advancing a specific set of goals. This is where the term useful idiot comes from. As long as a particular journalist can channel the narrative competently, she's hired. As long as the politician will follow the directives of his sponsor and vote yes on a bill like TPP, he'll get big campaign donations. As long as the professor infuses SJW talking points into his lectures, he gets tenure. These individuals have enough intelligence to do their jobs at a standard level, but that is secondary to their usefulness.

Growing up in America, you come to believe that people advance through their merit and ideas, but if you start examining these institutional positions and what allows individuals to rise to the top, you realize that their merit and ideas were only secondary. They were hired because those one level above found them to be useful, and no more. Intelligence is optional, and only necessary if the job demands it, but far more important is the ease of which they can be controlled to help usher in a pre-determined goal.[115]

In Europe and the Anglosphere, especially, these are the people that the masses are supposed to look up to and refer to as experts and authorities on every single matter of significance. However, these people are just useful idiots for their masters and employers. An astute believer needs to look at agendas, interests and incentives. Who owns the mass media organisations? The government policies that are being advocated, from wars to regulations and taxes, serve whose interests? Do you know that 90% of the media in the United is owned by a mere six

---

[115] http://www.rooshv.com/the-elites-are-not-smarter-than-you (Accessed Dec 15, 2016)

corporations?[116] Have a look at the article cited below and you will see all the connections and special interests involved.

The Agenda of the Left and the Media

So what, exactly, is the agenda? What are all these corporations, media organisations, career politicians, academics etc. working towards? The simple answer is control, to one degree or another. Some of them would like to go as far as creating some form of one world government.[117] Some of them would like to merely have control over the economy so that they can profit perpetually without having to worry about competition. Some of them would like to control the public discourse because they are too insecure and immature to handle criticism and disagreement. These desires for various forms of control are of course connected and overlap.

The desire to control the economy, in connection to these other forms of control, has led to the emergence of a new type of economy: corporatism. I say "new" because people in Europe and the Anglosphere are trained and educated to think of economic systems as either capitalist or socialist/communist. In

---

[116] http://www.wakingtimes.com/2015/08/28/the-illusion-of-choice-90-of-american-media-controlled-by-6-corporations/ (Accessed Dec 16, 2016)
[117] The new phase of the culture war is globalism vs nationalism: are people's interests best served by the nation state or by supranational organisations like the European Union and the United Nations? I first wrote about this after the United Kingdom voted to leave the EU: http://mahdinnm.blogspot.com/2016/06/the-globalists-and-nationalists.html (Accessed Dec 22, 2016) Just as they have been used by the left in individual Anglosphere and European countries, Muslims have also been used by the globalists to advance their cause.

the briefest terms, capitalism means that the means of production are in private hands, while communism means that the means of production are in government hands. Based on that definition, the countries of Europe and the Anglosphere are capitalist countries. However, what is often ignored or simply not understood is that the private companies that control the means of production are very closely allied to the government. According to Benito Mussolini, corporatism *is* fascism; the corporations are in bed with the government, writing out all the rules and regulations in order to stifle and snuff out the competition.

The best book on this topic, to my knowledge, is *Liberal Fascism* by Jonah Goldberg, which basically presents and deftly argues the thesis that so-called "far right" political parties and movements, including Mussolini's fascists and Hitler's Nazis (i.e. national socialists), are products of the left and not the right. Big government is always a product of the left. For example, prior to the outbreak of war in 1939, it was normal in the American press to draw comparisons between Hitler, Mussolini and Franklin D. Roosevelt. Isn't the media interesting?

An example of how corporations and useful idiots, with most likely the best of intentions, work together to implement corporatism is provided in the chapter on liberal fascist economics. Goldberg gives the example of a regulation being issued by the American government that stipulates that all "large" companies must have disabled access in all of their facilities, e.g. factories, warehouses, showrooms etc. On the surface, this sounds very kind and caring. The outcome will make lives easier for disabled persons, whether customers or employees. Prominent voices in the media and academia will support it and promote it. But how will the big corporations view this? Will these evil behemoths of "capitalism" be shaking in their tube socks? They most assuredly will not. Goldberg gives the example of Coca-Cola and Pepsi. The CEO of Coca-Cola will read the new regulation and smile as soon as he remembers that the CEO of Pepsi is reading the exact same document. Coca-Cola and Pepsi are huge, multinational companies, selling millions of units every day all over the world. To cover the costs of implementing the regulation, e.g. provide ramps, toilets, escalators etc., all they have to do is increase the prices of their products by a fraction of a cent, an amount so negligible that customers won't even notice. Furthermore, large corporations like Coca-Cola and Pepsi already have their own internal compliance departments, i.e. offices full of accountants and lawyers and other office workers who can dedicate all their time to making sure every new regulation is complied with. These large companies can also afford lobbyists, who spend all their time in Washington or Brussels and every other seat of power lobbying members of Congress, senators, EU commissioners etc. for the rules and regulations that favour them.

Goldberg then asks you to think about something completely hidden in all of this. It's just like Henry Hazlitt says in his book *Economics in One Lesson*:[118] economics is about faith in the unseen. What is unseen in this whole process is what happens to a small,

---

[118] https://infogalactic.com/info/Economics_in_One_Lesson (Accessed Dec 16, 2016)

regional company that is trying to work its way up to the level of the corporations. Imagine you are the owner of a state-wide soft drinks company and one day you hope to see eyeball to eyeball with Coca-Cola and Pepsi. You are quickly expanding but you are not a large company yet,[119] but if you hire just a few more people you will be, and the above regulation will immediately apply to you. Due to the fact that you only have facilities within your own state, as opposed to all over the world, your compliance costs will be nowhere near that of Coca-Cola and Pepsi, but it will still be very expensive, relatively speaking. Your market is only your home state, so you can't pass the expenses onto your customers because you would risk losing them. You would have to raise the price considerably to cover the costs. Furthermore, once you cross that threshold and legally become a large company, you will need your own compliance department. You will have to start hiring lawyers and accountants, which will be another massive expense. Becoming a large company could actually bankrupt you, and therefore it becomes safer to simply stop expanding and stop hiring. Just like that, the dream of one day competing with Coca-Cola and Pepsi dies.

When I first read this, it had me thinking. If the United States is such a "capitalist", "free market" economy, as the left always whines, why are there only two major soft drinks companies? Why are there only three major car manufacturers? Why are there are only a handful of media companies, movie studios, banks, fast food restaurants and so on and so forth? Why has it

---

[119] http://smallbusiness.chron.com/determines-small-business-vs-large-business-20302.html (Accessed Dec 16, 2016)

115

been this way for decades? Where *is* the competition? The answer is right there in Goldberg's book. America (as well as the rest of the Anglosphere and Europe, to varying degrees) is not a free market economy. It is a corporatist economy. It is crony capitalism, or as John Stossel aptly puts it, *crapitalism*.[120] Blaming the "free market" and "capitalism" every time something goes wrong with the economy is like blaming "Islam" for everything that has gone wrong or everything bad that a Muslim has done for the past century.[121]

---

[120] http://townhall.com/columnists/johnstossel/2014/07/02/crapitalism-n1857887 (Accessed Dec 16, 2016) Every year, corporatism/crapitalism is celebrated at the World Economic Forum in Davos, Switzerland. Daniel Hannan deftly describes it here: https://capx.co/davos-is-a-corporatist-racket/ (Accessed Dec 16, 2016). Based on everything that has been discussed in this chapter, it should come as no surprise that prominent spokesmen for Islam in the west have also been to Davos: https://www.weforum.org/events/world-economic-forum-annual-meeting-2015/sessions/religion-pretext-conflict/ (Accessed Dec 19, 2016).

[121] Most of the ten planks of Karl Marx's *Communist Manifesto* have been implemented in the United States, the most notable of them being a monopolistic central bank, i.e. the Federal Reserve: http://laissez-fairerepublic.com/tenplanks.html (Accessed Dec 17, 2016). One can also watch this video in which economist Milton Friedman illustrates the growth of US government regulations from 1936 to 1980: https://www.youtube.com/watch?v=15XVci0BTdw (Accessed Dec 17, 2016) Likewise, European colonialism of the Muslim heartlands, especially intellectual and scholarly centres like the Levant and Egypt, ruined the Islamic education system and more or less abolished the judiciary. Examples of this can be found in the book *Kubrā al-Yaqīniyyāt al-Kawniyyah* by Imam Muḥammad Saʿīd Ramaḍān al-Būṭī. Regulating the economy and needlessly intervening in productive activity causes economic problems, just as ruining the Islamic education system will produce ignorant Muslims who say and do stupid things, so it is indeed rich to destroy something and then blame the consequences on that which has been destroyed.

Where do Muslims in the Anglosphere fit in?

Muslims are a minority in terms of their religion, as Christianity is the religion of the majority. Racially, the vast majority of Muslims worldwide come from non-white countries, such as in Africa, the Middle East, the Indian subcontinent and south-east Asia. In the United States, only 30% of Muslims describe themselves as white.[122] Therefore, not only theologically but racially Muslims are a Minority in the Anglosphere.

Being a minority, and having minorities within that minority, means that Muslims are a useful tool for the politicians that seek control and have a psychological need to feel important. The narrative put forward by the mainstream media and the politicians is that the majority (whites, Christians, and particularly males) represents some sort of oppressive establishment, while every minority is somehow oppressed, whether it is women,[123] blacks, Hispanics, Muslims, Jews, homosexuals etc.[124] Therefore, it is both politically and psychologically beneficial for these narcissists and control-seekers

---

[122] http://www.people-press.org/2011/08/30/section-1-a-demographic-portrait-of-muslim-americans/ (Accessed Dec 17, 2016)
[123] Technically not a minority, but feminism has had a huge impact on Anglosphere culture: http://mahdinnm.blogspot.com/2016/07/where-did-generation-special-snowflake.html (Accessed Dec 17, 2016)
[124] Please see this blog post for further details: http://mahdinnm.blogspot.com/2016/10/cultural-marxism.html (Accessed Dec 17, 2016)

to claim that they care about these groups and to pretend to promote their causes, Muslims included.[125]

The three verses from the Qur'ān that are quoted at the beginning of this chapter are a reminder that there is no such thing as a "pro-Islam" unbeliever. Because people on the left say nice things about Islam and Muslims, it doesn't mean that they are "pro-Islam" while people on the right, such as Breitbart News, Infowars, Paul Joseph Watson etc. are "anti-Islam". The truth is that all of them are anti-Islam. They only differ in their degrees of dislike and how they express it. Paul Joseph Watson expresses his dislike verbally, in YouTube videos and articles. Hillary Clinton and Barack Obama express it by bombing and destabilising Muslim countries, thereby killing large numbers of Muslims or forcing them to become refugees.

It should also be kept in mind that the verses quoted above make it clear that Islam will be hated and Muslims will be rejected *regardless* of what Muslims do. Even if every Muslim on earth were incredibly righteous and pious, clean and disciplined, hardworking and respectful, they would still be hated by the

---

[125] The close relationship between Muslims and the left can also be attributed to the Cold War, in which many Arab countries allied themselves with the Soviet Union while the United States remained allied with Israel. In the 2000s, during the presidency of George W. Bush, it was mainly leftist groups that protested against the Iraq war, protests that were often coupled with pro-Palestine protests. However, being united with the left on one cause or issue does not automatically mean that we agree with them on every cause or issue, or even a majority of issues. The Respect Party in the United Kingdom is a perfect illustration of this: https://infogalactic.com/info/Respect_Party (Accessed Dec 17, 2016)

majority of humanity. Muslims in the Anglosphere, and worldwide, unfortunately and especially nowadays, are constantly associated with terrorism and rape. A Muslim reader might respond right now and say, 'That's because of the media!' That's interesting. Is that the same media who told you that Donald Trump was a racist and would never be elected president? Is that the same media who told you that Saddam Hussain had weapons of mass destruction? Is that the same media that peddles the myth of anthropogenic climate change? Is that the same media who tells you that to be against the European Union is racist and xenophobic? Either you trust the mainstream media or you don't. Or to put it differently, you can't blame them and at the same time have unflinching faith in them. Furthermore, ISIS is not a myth. 1400 white girls being raped by mainly Pakistanis in Rotherham alone is not a myth.[126] Unbelievers have additional reasons for disliking Muslims, and Muslims can only blame themselves.

The difference between the right and the left in how they deal with Muslims is that the former don't mince their words. They don't hide the fact that they dislike Islam. They're honest, and sometimes brutally so. The left, on the other hand, pushes this narrative that all minorities, including Muslims, are welcome and respected, and that anyone who says speaks against Islam or Muslims, even if it about terrorism or rape, is simply a racist or

---

[126] https://infogalactic.com/info/Rotherham_child_sexual_exploitation_scandal (Accessed Dec 17, 2016) Oddly enough, because of political correctness, the mainstream media has not fully reported on the thousands of cases of Pakistani males raping white girls in the UK and politicians have been slow, to say the least, in doing anything about the problem.

"Islamophobe". This is the culture of political correctness, or cultural Marxism.[127]

Political correctness is a huge problem and for several reasons. It is the tyranny of the lie. For Muslims, the core of it is the slogan "Islam means peace" or "Islam is a religion of peace". This is something that the authorities warned about in the 1960s, namely Imam Muḥammad Saʿīd Ramaḍān al-Būṭī in his book *Fiqh as-Sīrah* and Imam Wahbah az-Zuḥaylī in his book *Athār al-Ḥarb fī al-Fiqh al-Islāmī*. Islam is more than just a "religion", i.e. merely a system of faith and worship; it is also a system of governance.[128] The Messenger of Allah, may Allah bless him and grant him peace, was always a Messenger of Allah, calling people to faith, but he was also a political ruler in Madīnāh, the first Dār

---

[127] http://mahdinnm.blogspot.com/2016/10/cultural-marxism.html (Accessed Dec 22, 2016) In summary, cultural Marxism is an attempt to bring about communism (i.e. complete government control) via culture and the institutions as opposed to violent revolution. The end game is to make each and every individual dependent on the state, and to achieve this the individual has to be detached from traditional sources of support, such as one's family and one's local or religious community. This means that both the nuclear family and religion have to be destroyed. In Europe and the Anglosphere, the religion that must be destroyed is Christianity because it is the religion of the majority, and therefore Islam and Muslims, being the largest minority religion, are being used and exploited to undermine Christianity. As a Muslim in the Anglosphere, you should always be suspicious of any unbeliever who makes the assumption that you would be offended by the sight of a Christmas tree or hearing the words "Merry Christmas". This person is seeking to use you. First of all, you do not want to be someone who is easily offended. Secondly, you do not want to be someone who then complains to the government about being offended. And Allah knows best.

[128] For a detailed exposition of this matter, please see: http://mahdinnm.blogspot.com/2016/10/religion-of-peace.html (Accessed Dec 18, 2016)

al-Islām, or abode of Islam, to which he and his Companions had migrated from Makkah. Makkah had become Dār al-Ḥarb, or the abode of war, i.e. a land or territory in which Muslims are persecuted.[129] Once in Madīnah, the Muslims had a system of governance, a territory that they ruled over and community that lived under that rule, all of which needed to be defended and not just verbally but physically. This is why *jihād* was legislated. This is why all the battles between the Muslims and unbelievers took place after the migration, or Hijrah, to Madīnah. Therefore, Islam has rules and laws of governance and they include rules and laws concerning warfare. Islam is not a religion of peace and it is not a religion of war. Rather, Muslims, like any nation, have interests and they are legislated to fight in order to protect and maintain those interests. What Imam al-Būṭī and Imam az-Zuḥaylī warned about back in the 1960s was that people in the west, the right and the left, would seek to distort and pervert everything that is summarised above. To begin with, they would promote the notion that Islam is all about terrorism, tyranny and hatred. In other words, Islam is the same as ISIS. While Muslims are trying to formulate a response to this, someone else would promote the notion that Islam is a religion of peace and love and would never go to war unless attacked completely unannounced.[130] In other words, Islam is a big white, fluffy teddy

---

[129] Please see this article for more details: http://mahdinnm.blogspot.com/2011/04/abodes-of-earth.html (Accessed Dec 18, 2016)

[130] A Muslim ruler, like any sensible rule, keeps his eyes and ears open to any potential threat and will launch pre-emptive strikes if and when necessary. Please see the blog post "Religion of Peace", cited above, for further details.

bear. The truth lies somewhere in the middle, but the discourse in the Anglosphere is set up such that either someone says, "Islam is a religion of peace" (and such a person is deemed "pro-Islam"), or they do not (and such a person is deemed "anti-Islam"). This means that no honest discussion regarding terrorism or rape or anything a Muslim does, whether sanctioned by the Revealed Law or not, can ever take place. Anyone who goes off script and steps outside the "Islam means peace" Overton window can easily be dismissed as an "Islamophobe" or "racist".[131]

The left thus puts Muslims inside the politically correct bubble, in which they are lead down the garden path and allowed to think that any criticism of Islam or Muslims is just hate-filled bigotry that does not and should not merit a response.[132] No unbeliever is allowed to question why ISIS exists, or why terrorist attacks happen, or why white girls are being raped in various cities and towns. In fact, after every terrorist attack, the first thing the mainstream media and politicians talk about is an

---

[131] Another amazing irony is how people who say that Islam is *not* a religion of peace, in addition to being called racist etc., also receive death threats from Anglosphere Muslims: https://twitter.com/prisonplanet/status/707646895712301056 (Accessed Dec 21, 2016). Some Muslims will most likely argue that these threats are fabricated, but I know from experience the kinds of threats Anglosphere Muslims can make when you say something they disagree with. One can also visit Tommy Robinson's Twitter page to see the messages that he receives from Anglosphere Muslims.
[132] And sadly, it's common for Muslims in the Anglosphere to have an almost unbearable smugness about them: https://jurjis.wordpress.com/2016/10/20/anglosphere-islam-good-news-its-racist-and-vulgar/ (Accessed Dec 21, 2016)

"Islamophobic backlash". Will people now lash out at Muslims? People have just died. People's lives have been ruined, but the main concern is that Muslims might receive angry stares on the bus or a nasty comment from passersby. Does that not seem odd to you? Furthermore, the media and the politicians, as well as certain Muslims, will advance this startling notion that "Islamophobia" causes terrorism. In other words, because Muslims feel victimised, because they feel that they are the victims of bigotry and discrimination, which, ironically, may include being called a "terrorist" or Islam being called a "religion of violence", this contributes to Muslims committing acts of terrorism. Take a deep breath and mull that over.[133]

The truth about "Islamophobia"

A phobia is an irrational fear[134] and Islam is not a race. The word "Islamophobia" was invented by unbelievers in 1997[135] and inserted into the English lexicon. It has no basis in reality. Firstly, we know what Allah told us on this matter, namely the three verses quoted at the beginning of this chapter. Expecting

---

[133] As an example, have a look at this interview that took place after the Ohio State terrorist attack: https://www.youtube.com/watch?v=S4IhQuz2pzc (Accessed Dec 18, 2016). Notice how the Muslim academic blames "Islamophobia" first, then draws a baseless comparison with white supremacists and then denies that there is any need for Muslims in America to ask *themselves* why this is happening. Anglosphere Islam is not about introspection; it's about deflecting blame and denying responsibility. The left wants minorities to be in a perpetual state of victimhood, and Muslims have fallen right into that trap.

[134] https://en.oxforddictionaries.com/definition/phobia (Accessed Dec 18, 2016)

[135] https://infogalactic.com/info/Islamophobia (Accessed Dec 18, 2016)

unbelievers to like Islam and Muslims is like expecting a polar bear to meet a camel. Secondly, their dislike of and aversion to Islam is not necessarily irrational. They don't like terrorism. They don't like rape. They don't like the behaviour that they've seen from Muslims. They don't like the practice and therefore they've rejected the theory. Some of them have read the theory and they still don't like it. Even the unbelievers in Makkah, who saw the Messenger of Allah, may Allah bless him and grant him peace, in the flesh and testified to his honesty and trustworthiness, rejected him because, as Imam Muḥammad Mutawallī ash-Shaʿrāwī points out in his *tafsīr*,[136] they feared for their livelihoods. They were merchants and traders and their business largely relied on Arabs coming to Makkah from all over the Arabian Peninsula to pay homage to the idols. They feared that Islam would decimate their business.[137] As for Islam not being a race, racism is so abhorrent because one's race is an accident of birth. It is Allah's will and completely involuntary. No one *chooses* to be white or black or purple or whatever, and therefore to show hostility towards someone simply because the Lord created them a certain way is supremely unjust.[138]

---

[136] i.e. commentary on the Qurʾān

[137] And, of course, human beings have human desires. If they see Islam, or religion in general, as curbing their desires and passions, they will reject it. For a deeper understanding of how this works in the west, and especially the United States, have a look at this Harvard commencement speech by Russian philosopher Alexander Solzhenitsyn: http://www.orthodoxytoday.org/articles/SolzhenitsynHarvard.php (Accessed Dec 19, 2016)

[138] The beginning of this was Iblīs, or the Devil, refusing to prostrate to Adam because he was physically different, and therefore he regarded him as inferior.

Furthermore, one's skin colour does not influence one's thoughts and behaviour. There isn't a black way of thinking and acting as opposed to a white way of thinking and acting. Religion, on the other hand, is a conscious choice and the whole point of religion is to influence your thoughts, beliefs and behaviour. The thoughts, beliefs and behaviour that arise from that conscious, voluntary decision are therefore liable to be criticised, or even mocked. It is therefore a ridiculous idea to attempt to conflate race with religion.[139] They are mutually exclusive categories and to conflate them is simply to fall into the trap of political correctness, which in turn creates the politically correct bubble that so many Anglosphere Muslims live in.

Furthermore, religion has to be based on conviction. The only way that religion can be comparable to race is if religion, like race, is viewed as something that is simply inherited and inculcated within a person's identity, which would mean that it is merely imitation; a person is merely imitating his parents, his family, his community etc. He is not critically examining the doctrines of his inherited faith and *then* deciding to become a devout adherent. In *Jawharat at-Tawḥīd*, Imam al-Laqānī's well-known poem on theology, he states:

If one just mimics others in the Oneness of Allah (tawḥīd)

"**I am better than him. You created me from fire and You created him from clay.**" [al-ʾAʿrāf 7:12]
[139] This idea was put forward by one of the hippie converts within the last decade: https://www.youtube.com/watch?v=wtUc_ZZCECM (Accessed Dec 19, 2016). For further details on why Islam is not a race, please see: http://mahdinnm.blogspot.com/2015/10/islam-is-revelation-not-race-or-culture.html (Accessed Dec 19, 2016).

His faith has not been freed of redundancy (tardīd)[140]

Faith that is based on mere imitation is worthless. Imitation is what culture is based on. It is something that is passed down from one generation to the next and its only claim to legitimacy is that it was practiced by people before. If any religion is classified as such it can be easily dismissed, or at the very least subjected to reform. Islam is revelation. Its theology and law are defined by objective standards and there are authorities in every age who defend and uphold those standards. Anyone who asks that their faith not be denigrated because it is "part of their identity" is most likely someone who has inherited their faith as part and parcel of their culture and never critically examined its doctrines.[141]

Also, expecting unbelievers not to denigrate or criticise Islam, or Muslims, goes against what Allah has said in His Book. There is absolutely no revelational basis for such an expectation. "Islamophobia" is a thoroughly false notion and has only served

---

[140] i.e. his faith is repeated again and again but without firm conviction, and thus it is redundant, and it will be subject to doubts and misgivings: http://mahdinnm.blogspot.com/2012/11/beneficial-notes-on-jawharat-at-tawhid.html (Accessed Dec 19, 2016)
[141] As a side note, and this will be discussed further in the next chapter, if religion is conflated with race and therefore becomes an intrinsic part of a person's identity, how does preaching one's religion to non-adherents not become a hate crime, or an act that is equivalent to racism? Preaching one's faith to someone else automatically implies that the other's person faith is false or at least deficient in some way. Those who are calling for this conflation are inadvertently calling for preaching, or *da'wah*, to be banned.

to couch Anglosphere Muslims within a false sense of security, such that they assume that any criticism of Islam or Muslims can just be dismissed and derided, regardless of whether it is baseless or thoroughly genuine.[142] However, the bubble of political correctness is starting to fade,[143] and the questions and criticisms from unbelievers are starting to come thick and fast. Crying "Islamophobia" or "racism" simply isn't going to wash anymore, and this will have a huge say in whether Islam survives in the Anglosphere. This will be discussed in the next and final chapter.

---

[142] For example, the genuine concerns of someone like Tommy Robinson: http://mahdinnm.blogspot.co.uk/2015/12/why-are-they-angry.html (Accessed Dec 19, 2016)

[143] As Cernovich explains in *MAGA Mindset*, a large part of Donald Trump's winning campaign, and I stress "winning", was based on disavowing political correctness.

Chapter 7: Does Islam have a future in the Anglosphere? Should you wait around to find out?

"The angels ask those they take while they are wronging themselves, 'What were your circumstances?' They reply, 'We were oppressed on earth.' They say, 'Was Allah's earth not wide enough for you to have made Hijrah (i.e. to have migrated) elsewhere in it?' The shelter of such people will be Hell. What an evil destination!" [an-Nisā' 4:97]

I'm writing this chapter on December 20, 2016. Donald Trump has just secured the presidency of the United States by winning the Electoral College. Yesterday, the Russian Ambassador to Turkey was shot dead by an ISIS-sympathising Turkish police office, several people were mowed down by an ISIS truck driver at a Christmas market in Berlin and three people were shot outside an Islamic centre in Zurich. Meanwhile, spokesmen for Islam in the west meet in Abu Dhabi to "talk" about how Islam is a religion of peace.[144]

Is this the new normal?

Why are Muslims living in Europe and the Anglosphere? Why are they living in Dār al-Kufr,[145] i.e. the abode of unbelief? The

---

[144] https://www.facebook.com/photo.php?fbid=10154715833661544 (Accessed Dec 20, 2016)
[145] Please see: http://mahdinnm.blogspot.com/2011/04/abodes-of-earth.html (Accessed Dec 20, 2016) Dār al-Kufr is any land that is ruled by unbelievers

general ruling for living in Dār al-Kufr is that it is *makrūh*, i.e. disliked, which means that one is not sinning for doing so but it is better not to. The justifications for living there are explained by Imam Wahbah az-Zuhaylī as follows:

'It is not permissible for a Muslim to reside in Dar Al-Kufr, especially if he fears tribulation for his religion, because in residing amongst them their multitude is increased, except in the case of, as Al-Māwardī has stated: "If it comes to be that he, and his family and people, are able to manifest their religion therein, it is not permissible for them to emigrate because the place in which he is in may become Dar Al-Islam."[146] This is the short answer.

'As for the detailed answer: residing in non-Islamic lands in order to seek knowledge or spread the Islamic call, or to strengthen the Muslims, or to earn and work,[147] or due to an excuse such as treatment for an illness, or because of captivity, or being prevented from residing in an Islamic country, is permissible in the Revealed Law. In this there

but Muslims are not persecuted therein. They can live there and openly implement their faith.

[146] This is the primary reason for living in Dār al-Kufr: to preach and teach Islam in the hope that the people become Muslim and thus the land becomes part of Dār al-Islām. This is how Islam is supposed to spread. However, in the United States at least, the number of Muslims is only growing due to Muslim immigrants and their children. The convert community is disappearing: https://imamluqman.wordpress.com/2017/09/11/why-american-muslim-convert-communities-could-be-headed-towards-extinction-by-imam-abu-laith-luqman-ahmad/ (Accessed Sept 29, 2017)

[147] This is a justification that many Muslims in the Anglosphere will give, but don't forget the caveat, which is that you mustn't fear tribulation for your religion. Furthermore, none of these justifications mean that it is permissible for a Muslim to *settle* in such lands. Rather, it is only permissible on a temporary basis.

is an Islamic benefit for the Muslims, which is that it is preferred for such a person to stay and remain rather than leave [the Muslims living there]. In other than these situations, residence is not allowed.'[148]

As for Europe and the Anglosphere in particular, what is often referred to as "the West",[149] the ruling from the authorities, since at least 2001,[150] has been that Muslims should leave. This started with the tribulation of Minority Fiqh, which was discussed earlier. If Muslims currently residing in Europe and the Anglosphere, and particularly the United States, have to resort to an entirely new set of laws, i.e. a new *fiqh*, because their lives there are difficult and they are finding it hard to manifest their faith and implement their Lord's commands, this is an indication that this part of Dār al-Kufr is turning into Dār al-Ḥarb, or the abode of war, which means a land in which Muslims cannot manifest their faith and implement their Lord's commands. Instead of compromising their faith and adjusting it to fit Anglosphere or European norms and customs, they have to leave and find somewhere to live in which they can manifest and implement their faith.

If Muslims were claiming, prior to 2001, that they were in the United States, or other parts of the Anglosphere or Europe, in order to preach and spread and Islam, the emergence of

---

[148] Ibid.

[149] I prefer terms like "the Anglosphere" because it also includes countries like Australia and New Zealand, which are geographically not in the west but certainly of the same culture.

[150] http://mahdinnm.blogspot.com/2011/01/fiqh-of-minorities-part-1.html (Accessed Dec 20, 2016)

Minority Fiqh revealed the truth of the matter. Instead of Westerners being drawn to and influenced by Islam, Muslims were instead being drawn to and influenced by Western culture and civilisation. The game was up and the authorities called foul.

Anglosphere civilisation, spearheaded by the United States, is the dominant civilisation at this point in human history, and it appears to be a civilisation that Muslims, whether immigrant or indigenous convert, have horribly failed to grasp.

If one wants to truly understand Anglosphere culture and jurisprudence, the best book is probably Daniel Hannan's *How We Invented Freedom*. Anglosphere civilisation is based on parliamentary representation, property rights and the rule of law, and the statement that the law is the "law of the land" is actually a reference to common law, which is set of laws that grow like a coral, each legal ruling that is given is based on precedent. This is the opposite of the European understanding of jurisprudence, largely based on the Napoleonic Code, which writes out all the laws first and then implements them. Daniel Hannan explains:

'What distinguishes the common law from the Roman law that predominates in Continental Europe and its colonial offshoots? Chiefly this. The Continental legal model is deductive. A law is written down from first principles, and then those principles are applied to a particular case. Common law, to the astonishment of those raised in the Roman or Napoleonic systems, does the reverse. It builds up, case by case, with each decision serving as the starting point for the next dispute. It applies a doctrine known to lawyers as *stare decisis*: previous judgments should stand unaltered, serving as precedent. Common law is thus empirical rather than conceptual: it concerns itself with actual judgments that have been handed down in real cases, and then asks whether they need to be modified in light of different circumstances in a new case.'[151]

Hannan then enumerates five properties that distinguish common law from civil law systems: the jury system, emphasis on private ownership and free contract, the notion that anything not expressly prohibited is legal, the invigilation of the law of the land is everybody's business,[152] the need for an ultimate popular tribunal to determine the law, because the law is national and not monarchical. This is the Parliament, which is still called the High Court of Parliament on certain formal occasions.[153]

I mention these points for two reasons. The first is that Muslims should understand how Anglosphere countries function, both culturally and legally, and that they are not the same as European countries. Secondly, as Hannan explains in his book, anyone who migrates to an Anglosphere country, regardless of race or religion, is expected to adhere to the abovementioned principles and qualities and hold them in the highest regard.

---

[151] *How We Invented Freedom & Why It Matters* (London: Head of Zeus, 2013), p.77
[152] For example, a policeman is a citizen in uniform, not an agent of the state.
[153] Ibid, p.78-80

After Ben Carson made his comments in late 2015 regarding a Muslim becoming president of the United States,[154] Hannan claimed that Carson was being political rather than theological, which is absolutely true, but I couldn't help but thinking that Hannan was merely talking past Carson. Carson's point was that he would be wary of a Muslim president because the US Constitution is incompatible with the Revealed Law of Islam. Any Muslim president would have to reject certain parts of the Revealed Law and grant ultimate supremacy to the US Constitution, and he would be accused of blasphemy by Muslims for doing so. Carson also points out that a follower of any other religion, even a Christian, would have to put the US Constitution above his religious beliefs. In his article on Carson, Hannan says:

'Will Muslim-Americans be similarly assimilated? I'm optimistic. There are plenty of passages in the Old and New Testaments that can be read as incompatible with giving your first loyalty to a secular republic, but Jewish and Christian Americans, for the most part, have learned how to compartmentalize their beliefs.'[155]

Hannan and Carson are saying the same thing; the only difference is the phraseology. In the Anglosphere, ultimate loyalty belongs to the secular republic. Religious beliefs have to be subjugated or compartmentalised. This is why quoting the "no religious test" clause of the US Constitution in refutation of Carson is pointless. There is no religious test because it is

[154] Please see: http://mahdinnm.blogspot.com/2015/09/ben-carson-is-right.html (Accessed Dec 21, 2015)
[155] http://www.washingtonexaminer.com/never-mind-muslims-...-can-a-catholic-be-president/article/2572743 (Accessed Dec 21, 2016)

presumed that the president has already subjugated his religious beliefs.

Also, the comparison between Muslims and Catholics comes up again, and it is indeed shocking that certain spokesmen for Islam in the west advocate that Muslims in the Anglosphere follow the example of the Catholics.[156] Daniel Hannan succinctly describes this comparison and what it will lead to:

'Were he writing today, Kenyon might have drawn a parallel, not with the Cold War, but with the status of Islam in the West. Like English-speaking Catholics in the early modern period, Muslims are often on the receiving end of a prejudice that is more political than religious in inspiration. Non-Muslims don't complain about the practice of hajj any more than Protestants used to complain about the practice of confession. Most anti-Muslim animosity has the same root as the older anti-Catholic animosity, namely the fear that devotees might, in the last analysis, be disloyal to their country. As John Locke, who believed in toleration for every Christian denomination except Roman Catholicism put it, "All those who enter into it do thereby *ipso facto* deliver themselves up to the protection and service of another prince."

'British Catholics eventually overcame these prejudices by making great play of their patriotism, praying ostentatiously for the monarch[157] of the day and flying the flag from their churches.[158] By the nineteenth

---

[156] http://www.csmonitor.com/Commentary/Opinion/2010/0916/Amid-mosque-dispute-Muslims-can-look-to-Irish-Catholics-for-hope (Accessed Dec 21, 2016)
[157] Hannan has a point: http://mosaicmagazine.com/picks/2014/12/british-jews-pray-for-the-queen-why-shouldnt-muslims/ (Accessed Dec 21, 2016)
[158] And this, too, is an issue: http://www.yorkshirepost.co.uk/news/tory-mp-urges-muslims-to-fly-union-flag-at-mosques-1-2443853 (Accessed Dec 21, 2016)

century, the charge of divided loyalties had been comprehensively refuted by the long lists of Catholics among Britain's war dead. In the popular phrase of the time, Catholics had "proved their loyalty". A similar process will probably take place among Muslims in the Anglosphere, who will eventually understand that even the most baseless accusations will be answered patiently and courteously.'[159]

Muslims in the Anglosphere will not only have to pray for the head of the state and fly the nation's flag in their masjids, but they will also have to fight and die in wars to prove their loyalty. This is what the Catholics did because this is how things work in the Anglosphere. It's worth having a second look at Imam Wahbah az-Zuhaylī's ruling on residing and taking citizenship in Dār al-Kufr:

This is also the case because citizenship results in one being bound to certain requirements that may contradict the principles of Islam and its rulings, such as taking part in fighting Muslims or non-Muslims, and adhering to certain legal responsibilities that Islam has not affirmed.[160]

We are not supposed to join their armies and fight in their wars, but this is the next step if Muslims want to be "enfranchised". In the Anglosphere, being a citizen is not merely a case of bearing a passport. Rather, one's loyalty to the state, or to the crown, has to be the first loyalty, and this is especially the case in the United States. Americanism is effectively a meta-religion; every religion is subservient to it. Every scripture and holy book is subservient to the US Constitution. The Catholics in America, far from being

---

[159] *How We Invented Freedom*, p.38
[160] http://mahdinnm.blogspot.com/2011/04/abodes-of-earth.html (Accessed Dec 22, 2016)

an example for Muslims to follow, should be seen an example of how religions are watered down and subsumed when they take up residence in the Anglosphere. The watering down of Islam since 9/11, as discussed above and manifested in those four monstrosities, is actually par for the course when it comes to religion in these countries. This is the way things are set up, and Muslims would have to be incredibly knowledgeable, righteous, hard-working, tenacious and vigilant to have any hope of altering such an arrangement. What has happened over the better part of the last two decades has proved beyond any doubt that they are not.

That's the theory behind why Muslims should not be in the Anglosphere and why Islam will not and cannot survive there intact. One way or another, it will dissolve into the Anglosphere mainstream, and it appears that this process, which is well on its way, will finally be completed when large numbers of Anglosphere Muslims join the armies of their respective countries and die in wars. As for the practice, this is making matters far, far worse for Muslims, and we could narrow this down to four major areas: education, etiquette, terrorism and rape.

Education

As indicated in the chapter on the importance of the Arabic language, Anglosphere Muslims have not followed the path of previous non-Arab Muslim nations by learning Arabic, setting up seminaries and universities and then producing theologians and scholars who write significant books in Arabic and thus contribute to Islam's scholarly and intellectual legacy. An Anglosphere Muslim reading this might complain and say that seminaries and universities are long-term projects and that more time is needed, but the people who are revered as "scholars"[161] in the Anglosphere are not reproducing themselves. Instead of dedicating a large chunk of their time to conveying their knowledge to a select group of advanced students, they're touring the world giving talks. These advanced students, if they existed, would be teaching lower level students and there would be a system in place, but this isn't the case. This means that in terms of basic Islam knowledge, i.e. the most basic law and theology, Anglosphere Muslims are woefully behind the pace. Salvation being by faith alone and not dependent on deeds in any way, which is fundamental to orthodox, Sunni faith, is an alien concept to Anglosphere Muslims, even those who consider themselves educated and well-read, and this suffices as proof for what I am saying.[162] As for ignorance of basic legal matters, a

---

[161] I use quotation marks because for whatever knowledge they have, they still can't be compared to the scholars of the Muslim heartlands, not in knowledge, not in written legacy and certainly not in the production of students.

[162] As I mentioned earlier, not discussing this particular creedal point could have other reasons, such as fear of offending cultists, but both fear of offending cultists and simply not knowing or understanding this point lead to a deeper problem, which is insecurity with regards to one's faith. As a Muslim on this earth, not just in Dār al-Kufr or in the Anglosphere per se, you have to not only be prepared to be offended, but you have to be prepared to offend others, whether you mean to or not. If you fall into the trap of trying to impress or please people, even your parents, or at the very least not cause offense, your reason for being alive more or less ceases to be. What you do instead is you live of life of defense, constantly apologising and censoring yourself. You are essentially waiting to die, but you will be spiritually and emotionally dead long before you are physically. This is the state of people

good example would be the insistence of Muslim women in the Anglosphere to wear the full face veil, or *niqāb*, at all times, even at banks, airports or other situations in which they are asked to identify themselves. Unbelievers complain, and rightfully so, but the Muslim response is to play the victim.[163]

Furthermore, while there is a stress on reading works of western literature and philosophy and so forth, there is a blind spot when it comes to understanding Anglosphere culture as it is at present and where it came from. The key reason for this appears to be the disconnection from the authorities. For example, if Muslim leaders in the Anglosphere had heeded the words of Imams Wahbah az-Zuḥaylī and Muḥammad Saʿīd Ramaḍān al-Būṭī regarding the "religion of peace" scam, a warning that was first given in the 1960s, they would have avoided the trap of political correctness, become aware and vigilant and understood how unbelievers in the Anglosphere plot and plan to undermine Islam, and thus monstrosities like the Mardin Declaration would have never happened. Secondly, if, as an Anglosphere Muslim,

---

who just go along to get along, and listening to them, whether in speeches, interviews or whatever, or being in the presence of their followers, who will have automatically picked up this toxic mindset, will bring you down and make you stressed, anxious and depressed. If you are a strong, confident believer, they will *not* like you, because they will simply not understand you. Please protect yourself. Focus on pleasing your Lord, not people.
[163] This is discussed in detail in this article: https://jurjis.wordpress.com/2016/08/08/anglosphere-islam-when-muslim-activists-are-ignorant-of-the-revealed-law/ (Accessed Dec 25, 2016) Out of sheer ignorance, Anglosphere Muslims are placing strictures upon themselves where none exist. The victim mentality and sense of entitlement will be discussed further in the next section.

you're not going to follow the advice of the authorities, you could at least rely on your *own* knowledge and experience of growing up and living in such countries. You can't state the testimony of the faith and then lose your street smarts. You have to keep your eyes and ears peeled for hustlers and charlatans. Thirdly, even if your street smarts fail you, you should at least be able to take advice from the Lord's Revelation and understand that unbelievers will never like and accept you. If they appear to be doing so, there is an agenda behind it.

Right now, especially after the events of 2016, the protective cover of political correctness is coming off. After decades of having the luxury of brushing aside any question or criticism, no matter how genuine, as racist and Islamophobic, Muslims in the Anglosphere will now have to answer these questions and criticisms, and they will be woefully unprepared, firstly because of the protective bubble itself and secondly because they never thought that the bubble would pop, or realised that they were even in one.[164] In the last year, this bubble completely prevented

---

[164] The fatal flaw of the left is that instead of trying to convince their opponents of the veracity of their arguments and opinions, they shame them into silence and do their best to censor them. This is done by calling them names (e.g. racist, sexist, bigot, xenophobe etc.) and even threatening their jobs and careers. The obvious outcome is that people on the right refrain from expressing their opinions and arguments. Those on the left then make the fatal mistake of assuming that that the non-expression of these opinions means their non-existence, while in actual fact, those opinions are brewing and simmering under the surface, kept warm by flames of bitterness and resentment. After the 2015 UK General Election, in which the Conservative party surprisingly won because polls indicated a tight race, Janet Daley made this observation: http://www.telegraph.co.uk/news/general-election-2015/11594760/The-Tories-won-the-general-election-my-faith-in-the-British-

Muslim leadership in the Anglosphere from anticipating the election of Donald Trump, as well as the British vote to leave the European Union. Instead, Muslim leaders, just like the mainstream media and the left, assumed that it was nothing more than noise generated by "low-information" racists and bigots. Then the "unthinkable" happened.[165]

Socialism/communism/leftist ideology is dehumanising. What distinguishes us from animals is the blessing of intellect. We are able to think and rationalise and not just react to stimuli in some perfunctory manner. Human beings have motives, incentives and interests, and are able to devise plans and methods for achieving and protecting those interests. Therefore, to presume that 60 million people in the United States, i.e. those who voted from Mr Trump, or the 17.4 million Britons who voted to leave the European Union, did so for no other reason than that they are stupid, or ignorant, or gullible, or just racist and xenophobic and full of hate, is to dehumanise them, because one is denying them any intellectual faculty, that which distinguishes them from reptiles and the rest of the animal kingdom. Then, by stripping these people of their humanity, one strips oneself of one's own humanity, because one is failing to use one's own intellect and capacity to learn to even attempt to understand why millions of

---

people-was-entirely-justified.html (Accessed Dec 23, 2016) All the "undecideds" were actually conservative voters hiding their opinions. Just like conservative opinions, opinions and criticisms about Muslims have not gone away simply because they've been silenced and dismissed for so many years.
[165] I discussed this on my blog just before the election: http://mahdinnm.blogspot.com/2016/11/spirit-cooking-and-inhuman-reign-of-lie.html (Accessed Dec 24, 2016)

people chose to vote in such a way.[166] I defy any Muslim in the United Kingdom to label all the fishermen who voted to leave the European Union racist and bigoted,[167] or the thousands of Americans who have lost loved ones due to murderous illegal aliens.[168] And of course, there are other reasons for voting for Mr

---

[166] I highly recommend this article by Brendan O'Neill: http://www.spiked-online.com/newsite/article/brexit-this-was-a-vote-against-bigotry-not-for-it/18514#.WF6dV_l97IU (Accessed Dec 24, 2016) In the first paragraph he states, 'A bigot is someone who is so "obstinately and blindly devoted to his own church, party, belief, or opinion" that he comes to loathe those of a different church, party, belief or opinion. Which raises a pressing and intriguing question: in Britain's EU referendum debate, who, really, are the bigots?'

[167] There are two major documentaries about why Britain should leave the European Union, namely *Brexit: The Movie*, which is the argument from the right and includes people like Daniel Hannan and Nigel Farage, and *Lexit*, which is the argument from the left and includes people like George Galloway and Tony Benn. British fishermen appear in both documentaries, as their trade had been absolutely devastated by the EU's Common Fisheries Policy. Please read this article for details and statistics: http://www.telegraph.co.uk/business/2016/10/01/what-the-uks-fishing-industry-wants-from-brexit/ (Accessed Dec 24, 2016)

[168] For example: http://www.theremembranceproject.org/home.html and http://www.ojjpac.org/memorial.asp (Both accessed Dec 24, 2016) Furthermore, is it really wrong to expect priority treatment as a citizen in one's own country?

Trump, such as the economy, terrorism[169] and the fact that he is not Hillary Clinton.[170]

In summary, if you fail so spectacularly to understand the culture and society in your country of residence, you don't survive.

---

[169] This will be discussed later in the chapter, but to assume that being worried about terrorism is "Islamophobic" is beyond ridiculous. Unbelievers in the Anglosphere are especially worried about the fact that the vast majority of terrorists are only identified as such after the fact, i.e. after they've committed an atrocity and died in the process. Friends and family members come forward and say that they are completely shocked and that they "had no idea" that so-and-so would ever do such a thing. Unbelievers then ask, and rightly so: how can we then tell who is a threat and who isn't? If there were some telltale signs, some red flags, some indication or other, that would help a lot.
[170] This is an interesting poll: http://www.redstate.com/brandon_morse/2016/08/26/poll-majority-people-voting-trump-just-voting-clinton/ (Accessed Dec 24, 2016). It is truly remarkable that Muslim leadership in America was more or less oblivious to the overwhelming corruption of Hillary Clinton, and that this would contribute to people voting for Donald Trump. The assumption was always that Trump was the worst possible option (see http://seekershub.org/blog/2016/11/donald-trump-president-muslim-reactions/, accessed Dec 24, 2016), even though Jill Stein, the Green Party candidate and ardent leftist, had to admit that Clinton's threat of military action against Russia, a nuclear power, and her policies in general, made her a much scarier option than Trump: http://www.realclearpolitics.com/video/2016/10/12/jill_stein_hillary_clintons_declared_syria_policy_could_start_a_nuclear_war.html (Accessed Dec 24, 2016) We also shouldn't forget that Clinton's policies towards the Islamic world, i.e. those she supported as a senator and those she implemented as Secretary of State, were not exactly pro-Muslim: http://mahdinnm.blogspot.com/2016/08/actions-speak-louder-than-words.html (Accessed Dec 24, 2016)

Manners

Having a poor education and poor understanding of the world around you has consequences, especially if you have fallen into the liberal progressive political correctness trap and believe that no criticism of your religion or your community is justified and is instead a manifestation of racism and Islamophobia. The result of being so easily duped and fooled by the left is that you adopt the victim mentality that they desire of you, and thus you join the ranks of the perpetually aggrieved and offended, forever subjected to one form or another of injustice and hostility.

Hypersensitivity has never been an attractive character trait. Hypersensitive people have no control over their emotions and give off an incredibly negative vibe. Being in their presence brings you down and makes you feel stressed and anxious. Trying to rationalise with them only makes matters worse, because validation for their emotions is what they seek, not solutions to any perceived problem or a different perspective. The victim mentality is attractive and appealing because it absolves the individual of all personal responsibility and instead places the blame for that individual's failures on "society", or "the system", or "patriarchy", or "white male privilege" or whatever.

This is not to say that racism and discrimination don't exist. Rather, it is the mindset that is the problem. Blaming external factors for *all* of one's problems or failures is the essence of a slave mindset. It is completely disempowering. It tells you that there is nothing you can do. Just be miserable and look at everyone who is more successful than you or happier than you with the utmost envy, bitterness, vindictiveness and resentment, because what they are enjoying is the product of you being oppressed. It should be noted that for the left, life is a zero-sum game, which means that no one gets more unless someone else gets less, as if all wealth in this world is a pie that fell from heaven, and this is why they keep stressing equality, i.e. equality of outcome. The right sees life as a positive-sum game, i.e. the pie's size is not fixed, it can get bigger, and therefore equality of outcome is oppression.[171] Rather, equality of opportunity is what matters. Once you snap out of this and realise that you can work hard, depend on Allah, and make great changes in your life, the narcissists on the left will not be happy.[172]

---

[171] Inequality is always a side-effect of increased prosperity, as those who are more hardworking, industrious and creative will create more wealth for themselves. When governments try to impose equality of outcome, the process, or policy, involves taking from those more industrious people and giving it to those who are not, i.e. "tax the rich" as street protestors say, or "wealth redistribution", as the politicians put it. Such policies tend to redistribute people more than money, as the wealthy, who also happen to be rather clever, find ways and means of moving their money, their business, and even their own persons, elsewhere. Francois Hollande's 75% income tax on the wealthy in France is a typical, typical example. Equality is thus a side-effect of less prosperity.

[172] Dr Ben Carson, for example, is the ultimate success story. He was raised in poverty by his mother and is now one of the world's foremost neurosurgeons, one of a handful of people who have successfully separated conjoined twins and is the only person to have ever successfully separated Siamese twins joined at the back of the head. His story should be an inspiration to blacks in the United States, but Dr Carson is a Christian and a conservative, so do some research into how the left treats him. https://infogalactic.com/info/Ben_Carson (Accessed Dec 25, 2016)

This defeatist mindset comes with a strong sense of entitlement, and this in turn leads to bad manners. If you're always the victim, if the whole world is always against you, holding you down and never giving you what is rightfully yours, why not get angry and let the world know about it? On top of that, why not pay even closer attention and notice all the really subtle offenses that are done to you? For example, if Nike doesn't offer the words "Islam" or "Muslim" as a customisation option for your shoes, this must be because Nike thinks Muslims are violent or they simply don't want such words on their products.[173] If you apply for a job at a dental clinic and you don't wear a headscarf or even look remotely Muslim for the job interview, the first day at work, the second day at work, and then show up to work on the third day with a headscarf and get fired, that's "Islamophobic". We'll just conveniently ignore the fact that the employer had no idea you were a Muslim, or a "practising" Muslim, before that time.[174]

---

[173] http://madworldnews.com/muslim-big-demand-nike/ (Accessed Dec 25, 2016) Why any Muslim would want "Islam" or "Muslim" written on their shoes is curious enough, but notice how Nike was simply not given the benefit of the doubt. Instead, the Muslim assumed that they were being deliberately offensive. I found this article by typing "muslim sense of entitlement" on Google, which produced 462,000 results. There are articles and posts from Australia, New Zealand, Canada, the United States and the United Kingdom, so the trend exists throughout the Anglosphere.

[174] https://jurjis.wordpress.com/2016/08/08/anglosphere-islam-when-i-decide-to-be-practicing-so-do-you/ (Accessed Dec 25, 2016) This situation could have been caused by some of the idiotic career advise that Anglosphere Muslims pass around, which includes "Don't look like a Muslim at the job interview, or they might not hire you." Translation: "They might not like Muslims, so don't let them think you are one, or at least a committed one." But if I'm a Muslim and they don't like Muslims, why would I want to work for them? Would it not be better to go the interview and be very open about my faith? That would be

The victim mentality and sense of entitlement don't just create hypersensitive *defensive* behaviour. It also creates *offensive* behaviour, in which Anglosphere Muslims feel they have the right to instigate attacks against people, safe in the knowledge that they can claim to be the victim afterwards. This means that Anglosphere Muslims have, at times, started incidents with other minorities, such as West Indians in London,[175] and the majority white, Christian community.[176] For examples of general thuggery shown to white people by Anglosphere Muslims, I would recommend watching interviews and talks by Tommy Robinson,[177] or visiting his Twitter page.

In addition to the hypersensitive, defensive behaviour and the deplorable, offensive behaviour, Anglosphere Muslims also feel entitled to *pretend* that they have been attacked in order to "create awareness" of Islamophobia, or to stage incidents in which their supposed "attackers" actually have no choice but to take action against them. The aforementioned incident of the woman fired from the dental clinic for wearing a headscarf may have been staged, i.e. it might have been her plan all along to wear a headscarf *after* getting the job and working for a few days

---

a win-win situation. Either way, I would not end up working with people who are uncomfortable with me being a Muslim.

[175] https://jurjis.wordpress.com/2015/10/18/when-you-anger-other-minorities/ (Accessed Dec 25, 2016)

[176] The worst of this is the terrorism and the ongoing rape of underage white girls, in Rotherham, Rochdale, Bradford and several other places in the United Kingdom. This will be discussed in more detail later in this chapter.

[177] This is as good a place to start as any: http://mahdinnm.blogspot.com/2015/12/why-are-they-angry.html (Accessed Dec 26, 2016)

so as to provoke a response, and the Lord knows best, but the most well-known incident in recent memory of a deliberate set up is that of "clock boy" Ahmed Mohammed.

On the first day back at school after the fourteenth anniversary of 9/11, Ahmed Mohammed, a 14-year-old in Texas, brought a "homemade" clock to school that looked like a bomb.[178] Ahmed brought in his suspicious-looking device because he wanted to impress his engineering teacher, i.e. it was not part of any assignment, who rightly told him not to show it to anybody because it looked suspicious. He then brought it to his English class and it beeped during the lessons, which caused alarm. Eventually the police came and Ahmed did not fully co-operate with them, e.g. he didn't even ask them to speak to the engineering teacher, who could have vouched for him. Instead, he just kept repeating that it was a clock.

Ahmed and his family, along with the media and people like Barack Obama and Mark Zuckerberg, turned the incident into an example of "Islamophobia", but any decent research into the matter reveals that it was a deliberate ploy to make Ahmed look like a victim. Why would a Muslim bring a device that looks like a bomb into school the first day after the anniversary of 9/11? You can't blame students, teachers, police officers, or the society at large for associating Muslims with terrorism.[179] Daniel Hannan

---

[178] Please see this: http://mahdinnm.blogspot.com/2015/09/the-muslim-boy-who-cried-clock.html (Accessed Dec 26, 2016) and especially the video by Stefan Molyneux.

[179] I know. At this point, an Anglosphere Muslim reader might say that it's the mainstream media's fault, that the media blows things out of proportion,

has an interesting thought experiment: imagine a Muslim and a Christian sitting in a café. The Christian stands up and cries, 'Jesus Christ is my Lord and Saviour!' A few minutes later, the Muslim stands up and cries, 'Allahu Akbar!' How would the other customers react? In response to the former, they would most likely look up with bemused faces and then go back to their cakes and teas. After the latter, they'd all be on the floor ducking for cover or heading for the nearest exit. If you disagree, you're lying to yourself. Any sane Muslim knows that we have to watch our behaviour.

Another, more recent, deliberate setup was known YouTube prankster Adam Saleh claiming to be kicked off a Delta Airlines for nothing other than speaking Arabic, even though eye-witnesses, i.e. his fellow passengers, have stated that he and his colleague were actually shouting in Arabic and deliberately making a scene, and this was included in Delta's official statement on the matter.[180] The latest statement reads:

Upon landing the crew was debriefed and multiple passenger statements collected. Based on the information collected to date, it appears the customers who were removed sought to disrupt the cabin with provocative behavior, including shouting. This type of conduct is

---

exaggerates, lies etc. I repeat myself: so why do you believe them when they report on other people and other issues? Are they trustworthy or not? My point here is that the perception exists, whether you like it or not. If you want to blame westerners for blindly following the media and not doing research into Islam and terrorism, then you also have to blame yourself for not doing research into the European Union, climate change, Donald Trump etc.
[180] http://news.delta.com/updated-statement-customers-removed-disruptive-behavior (Accessed Dec 26, 2016)

not welcome on any Delta flight. While one, according to media reports, is a known prankster who was video recorded and encouraged by his traveling companion, what is paramount to Delta is the safety and comfort of our passengers and employees. It is clear these individuals sought to violate that priority.

The reader should also bear in mind that this took place within days of the Berlin terrorist attack, in which 12 people were killed and several others injured as a terrorist ploughed a truck through a Christmas market. It's safe to say that people in Europe and the Anglosphere were on extra high alert about terrorism in the days leading up to Christmas. To pull a stunt like this, especially at such a time, is reckless, insensitive and incredibly stupid. The fact that Saleh has a long catalogue of recorded pranks,[181] including pranks on airplanes, makes him look very much like the boy who cried wolf. Saleh also started a "Boycott Delta" hashtag, which has swept up the usual gullible celebrities, and thus there will be economic repercussions for his antics.[182] Actions like this do not help Muslims, or the image of Islam and Muslims, in the Anglosphere. When a wolf actually did come, the boy cried for help again but no one came, and he lost everything.

Other recent examples include Muslims claiming to be attacked by Donald Trump supporters since the election,[183] and a Muslim

---

[181] Pranking is also ḥarām, because of the risk involved and the damage it causes. Not everyone finds it funny, or even knows that it's a joke.

[182] http://www.breitbart.com/big-hollywood/2016/12/21/celebrities-vow-boycott-delta-youtube-hoaxster-adam-saleh-booted-flight/ (Accessed Dec 26, 2016)

[183] http://www.nydailynews.com/new-york/muslim-woman-reported-trump-supporter-attack-made-story-article-1.2910944 and

in Houston starting a fire in his local masjid on Christmas Day 2015, presumably to make it look like an anti-Muslim attack.[184] This does not bode well for the future.

Terrorism

Before going into the discussion, I need to lay down a definition. A Muslim terrorist, or an Islamic terrorist attack, has to be an attack in which a Muslim injures or kills someone in the name of Islam, e.g. they cry 'Allahu Akbar'. I say this because people will mention attacks and murders carried out by Christians, Jews, Hindus, atheists, communists etc. but the question is: are all these attacks carried out in the name of their respective religions and ideologies?

The second point is that of theology. Terrorist organisations and individuals are not adherents of Orthodox, Sunni theology, namely the three schools of Imam Aḥmad ibn Ḥanbal, Abū Hasan al-Ashʿarī and Abū Manṣūr al-Māturīdī.[185] A crucial doctrine that distinguishes Orthodox Islam from the cults and heretics is the doctrine of faith-based salvation, which has been mentioned before and I have pointed out that it is not taught or preached in the Anglosphere. At best, it is alluded to here and there but never fleshed out in any detail.

---

http://dailycaller.com/2016/12/21/stunner-anti-muslim-threat-at-university-of-michigan-was-a-huge-hoax/ (Both accessed Dec 27, 2016)
[184] http://www.chron.com/news/houston-texas/article/Houston-man-pleads-guilty-in-mosque-fire-10785703.php (Accessed Dec 27, 2016)
[185] Please see *Lawāmiʾ al-Anwār al-Bahiyah* by Imam Aḥmad as-Safarīnī (Beirut: al-Maktab al-Islāmī, 1411/1991) v.1 p.73

A common denominator of all of these terrorists is that they didn't exactly live pious, devout lives prior to committing their terrorist acts. As Daniel Hannan pointed out after the Charlie Hebdo attack, the standard terrorist background is: young, male, vain, angry, a history of petty crime and drug abuse, a yearning to be part of something bigger.[186] And there are other traits:

'Islamist gunmen, in terms of character, are not so very different from, say, Red Brigaders or Baader-Meinhof gangsters. We see the same traits again and again: narcissism, alienation, violent proclivities, a belief that you can see things more clearly than anyone else.'[187]

Hannan then mentions this:

'In 2008, a briefing note by MI5 was leaked to the Guardian. It concluded that "'far from being religious zealots, a large number of those involved in terrorism do not practise their faith regularly. Many lack religious literacy and could be regarded as religious novices."'[188]

How is this connected to theology? As mentioned before, the cults that run wild in the Anglosphere preach a doctrine of deeds-based salvation. In other words, being a Muslim is not going to get you into Paradise. You have to be a 51% good Muslim. If not, you will be lost for all eternity.

Let's picture a scenario here. A young man from a "cultural" Muslim family, living somewhere in the Anglosphere, reaches a

---

[186] https://capx.co/the-best-antidote-to-terrorism-is-ridicule/ (Accessed Dec 27, 2016)
[187] Ibid.
[188] Ibid.

point in life where he feels like he's going nowhere. He can't seem to hold down a job. He can't start a business. He's had no success in relationships. He has also never been a devout Muslim. He only prays occasionally and if he goes to the masjid, it's only on Eid and Fridays. He then decides to turn to His Lord, but he is also bitter about how his life has turned out so far. The media and the politicians constantly feed him the narrative of racism and Islamophobia, which pushes him into a victim mindset. It's comforting, because he doesn't have to blame himself for any of his problems or his failures.[189] He doesn't know what his true identity is, what his home country is, but he does know that he is a Muslim. Maybe Islam will give him a sense of identity. Maybe Islam will give his life some meaning and some structure.

The young man speaks English and maybe some Urdu, or Punjabi or Mirpuri, but no Arabic, and therefore he is restricted to the speakers, teachers, books and writings that are in those languages, and we have already explained how this is severely lacking when compared to the rich abundance of knowledge and wisdom that is found in the Arabic literature, which makes up more than 99% of all Islamic literature. Furthermore, those who do speak Arabic and have studied in the Muslim world are not focusing their attention on reproducing themselves and putting a

---

[189] If this young man is in the United Kingdom and has Pakistani parents, you could also add the "cultural dissonance" factor, i.e. the fact that he doesn't fully identify with his parents' culture and he doesn't fully identify with British/Anglosphere culture:
https://theodoredalrymple.wordpress.com/2015/12/24/the-gramscian-islamists/ (Accessed Dec 28, 2016)

system in place through which common believers can grow and develop in knowledge and in their faith in general.

The young man would start, like anyone else, by attending talks and lectures, and maybe move on to some courses. It will depend on him finding speakers who actually move on to the next step, which is not common amongst those who have emigrated from the Indian subcontinent.[190]

It is very likely that he will have to look outside his own community or religious grouping[191] and will most likely end up with cultists and political activists. As Hannan explains in his article, these people will validate his feelings of resentment, bitterness and alienation and give him that feeling that he is part of something bigger and that he can see things clearer than anyone else. But there's something else that Hannan doesn't

---

[190] Back in 1996, while teaching a class in Damascus on the true understanding of *jihād* in Islam that was based on a book he had written, Imam Muḥammad Saʿīd Ramaḍān al-Būṭī, may Allah have mercy on him, encouraged those attending the class to ask questions, because he was not just preaching or speaking but teaching a class. He then stressed that the benefit of preaching is that it wakes up people's religious fervour, it makes them more passionate about their faith, but if that fervour and passion is not accompanied by knowledge it can be dangerous and harmful. A recent example of this is a boy in Pakistan chopping off his own hand because he believed he had committed blasphemy, and his community praising him for doing so: http://www.bbc.com/news/world-asia-35341256 (Accessed Dec 28, 2016) Most Muslims in the United Kingdom are of Pakistani origin, and when Pakistanis refer to someone as a "scholar", more often than not they mean that the person is a skilled orator, not a teacher or author. Common Muslims, wherever they are, need opportunities in which they can ask questions, so that they can grow in knowledge and understanding and not just passion and fervour.

[191] Ar. *jamāʿah*, or 'jamaat' in Urdu

mention, and I would never expect him to as he is not a theologian, and it is the doctrine of deeds-based salvation. How is this young man now going to compensate for years and years of "not practicing", of missing prayers, missing fasts, maybe engaging in illicit things like fornication and drugs, and so on and so forth? What is he going to have to do to become that 51% good Muslim? Is he going to have to make up all those fasts and prayers? That's going to take a lot of time. This young man is angry, he's frustrated, he's bitter towards the society around him and at the same time he needs to do something to redeem himself. What could he possibly do?

I don't think I need to spell this out. A young man in this situation will easily fall prey to talk of martyrdom. He will be easily convinced, whether he meets these demons online or in person, that to save himself from eternal damnation he must sacrifice himself, and take some infidels with him in the process.

A situation like this is unspeakably sad. There are so many things that could have saved this man's life and that of others. Knowing and understanding faith-based salvation could have saved him. He could have learned that the Lord accepts him as he is, and all he had to do was repent and seek forgiveness. He could have been saved by teachers, who would have guided him, advised him and answered his questions. These things are lacking in the Anglosphere.

Moving on from the individual, unbelievers ask about the condemnation from the wider Muslim community. What are Muslims in the Anglosphere, as a community, doing about this?

Do they agree with such attacks? Do they condone them? Do they try to justify them? After the Ohio State terrorist attack in late 2016, mentioned in a footnote above, Tucker Carlson asked a Muslim professor about what the Muslim community was doing about terrorism committed by its members, and the Muslim professor did mention "Islamophobia" as "contributing" to terrorism.[192] What she says about "cultural homelessness" is the same as "cultural dissonance", but to blame a host country or culture for making an immigrant feel alienated is completely illogical. Don't move to America unless you want to become American. The immigrant has to adapt to the host. A new employee adapts to the company. A new convert adapts to the religion. No one looks at a group, religion, country, culture or whatever, decides to join it and then after doing so expects it to change and adapt to meet his own needs and desires. I mentioned above that alienation and bitterness contribute to terrorism, but that alienation and bitterness is not the fault of the host culture or nation. If you voluntarily move somewhere, you have to be prepared to adapt, not the other way around.[193]

---

[192] https://www.youtube.com/watch?v=xESAWKjnMkM (Accessed Dec 28, 2016)

[193] In the case of a refugee, someone who did not move to Europe or the Anglosphere voluntarily but was forced to do so because of war or a natural disaster, such a person should just be quiet and be grateful. Why complain about the only place that would grant you refuge? One should also look at the statistics that Donald Trump quoted when he announced his temporary ban on Muslim immigration to the US: https://www.donaldjtrump.com/press-releases/donald-j.-trump-statement-on-preventing-muslim-immigration (Accessed Dec 29, 2016) This does not bode well for the future.

This "politically correct" attitude towards terrorism has been a failure. In the same way that calling a disabled person "differently-abled" will never change that person's condition, labelling terrorist acts as simply "attacks" or "incidents" or claiming that they have nothing do with Islam, or Islam is a "religion of peace", is not going to change anything. This is just an expression of denial. Political correctness is now dying in the Anglosphere and Muslims living there, especially their leaders, appear to be woefully unprepared.[194]

Rape

Compared to terrorism, rape hasn't killed the same number of people, but it has probably destroyed a similar number of lives. 52 innocent people were killed on July 7, 2005, in London, while 1400 underage white girls were raped in the Yorkshire town of Rotherham[195] over a 25-year period, and it's still going on.[196] Again, political correctness has failed to protect innocent people while at the same time giving the perpetrators and their communities a sense of invulnerability, which in turn leads to arrogance and smugness, so much so that rape gangs openly and brazenly threaten victims and their families. The authorities, whether it is the police or the local council, won't do anything

---

[194] For more on the coming collapse of political correctness, please see: http://mahdinnm.blogspot.com/2016/11/spirit-cooking-and-inhuman-reign-of-lie.html (Accessed Dec 29, 2016)

[195] And it's not just Rotherham, but other towns and cities across the UK: https://infogalactic.com/info/Rotherham_child_sexual_exploitation_scandal (Accessed Dec 29, 2016)

[196] http://www.express.co.uk/news/uk/697583/Rotherham-abuse-scandal-child-grooming-gangs-industrial-scale-victims-CSE (Accessed Dec 29, 2016)

because being called a "racist" is apparently of greater concern than protecting children from rapists. Furthermore, just like terrorism, Muslim organisations and "leaders" have attempted to reframe the problem and make *themselves* the victim.[197]

The article referenced above highlights a major cultural difference between Pakistanis and the English, or indeed white people in the Anglosphere. Muslims may very well point out that there are paedophiles and child rapists amongst the white community, for example people like Jimmy Savile, and therefore paedophilia and child rape are not just a Muslim or Pakistani problem, so why pick on Muslims and Pakistanis? What's the difference? The difference is in the reaction. When white people learn about one of their own being a child rapist or paedophile, they immediately turn on that person, unless they themselves are somehow connected to the crime. Look at how Jimmy Savile went from hero to less than zero once news of his heinous crimes became undeniable. His memory, or what was good about it, was completely wiped.[198] Muslims, or Pakistanis, on the other hand, have active child rapists amongst them right now and they're not doing anything about it. This certainly gives the impression that

---

[197] http://www.express.co.uk/news/uk/615246/Rotherham-sex-scandal-Islamic-British-Muslim-Youth-boycott-South-Yorkshire-Police?_ga=1.199091119.1402442186.1478060913 (Accessed Dec 29, 2016)
[198] https://infogalactic.com/info/Jimmy_Savile_sexual_abuse_scandal (Accessed Dec 29, 2016) I also highly recommend this article: https://jurjis.wordpress.com/2014/09/10/england-the-coming-race-way-introduction/ (Accessed Feb 27, 2017)

Pakistanis, or Muslims in general, see nothing wrong with such behaviour. It's just part of their culture.[199]

So far on this topic, I've only talked about the United Kingdom, and not only because it is the Anglosphere country where the monstrosity is most prevalent, but also because the character of the British, or the English is particular, is not the same as other English-speaking people, especially Americans. To an outsider, Americans can come across as very strong and dominating, while the English can seem very quiet and passive. This is an illusion. Yes, the Americans are strong and dominating, but the English are actually slow to anger, which is not the same as being quiet and passive. Rape on an industrial scale of American white girls has not happened because Muslims would be killed or severely injured by American families, and very quickly.[200] There would be no deliberation or hesitation. Retribution would be swift and hard.[201] The English, on the other hand, take their time, but it does not mean they're not doing anything. Think of it this way. If

---

[199] I know from living in the United Kingdom and from friends who still live there that when Pakistanis molest their own, for example an imam of a masjid molests kids in a Qur'an class, that imam will not be disciplined. Instead, he will just be moved to another masjid. The fact that individuals molest little kids doesn't actually seem to invoke any sort of disgust or anger in them, and Allah knows best.
[200] https://jurjis.wordpress.com/2015/12/15/has-the-march-of-the-english-white-man-begun/ (Accessed Dec 29, 2016)
[201] This is how an American father reacts to his child being molested: http://www.dailymail.co.uk/news/article-2700872/My-son-saved-attackers-life-Father-pounded-admitted-child-molester-bloody-puddle-claims-son-stopped-stabbing-admitted-pedophile-death.html (Accessed Dec 29, 2016) I hope the reader notices that the father will not be charged for any crime. The police understand that he did what a father is supposed to do.

an American wants to get some undesirable person out of his swimming pool, he'll just forcibly remove him. An Englishman will save his energy and drain the pool instead. This applies to the police as well. American police have a reputation for being tough and even brutish, while British police are regarded as more cunning and conniving.[202]

What does this all mean? Pakistanis in the United Kingdom, and to an extent all Muslims in the Anglosphere, should not assume that there will be no payback for all the white girls, the thousands of white girls, that have been raped and abused over decades. Respect for females in general, especially white women and girls in this case, needs to be learned fast, but it looks like it's too late. One only has to read the works of people like Lloyd George or Hamilton Gibb regarding colonial Egypt to learn that the English are brilliant when it comes to planning, especially long-term planning.[203]

Conclusion

The conclusion to this chapter, and indeed the whole book, is that Islam in the Anglosphere does not have a bright future, or even a future at all. Muslims in the Anglosphere will eventually fall into one of three categories:

---

[202] The film *In the Name of the Father*, starring Daniel Day Lewis, which is based on the true story of the Guildford Four, illustrates very clearly how British police can operate.
[203] This was discussed by Imam Muḥammad Saʿīd Ramaḍān al-Būtī in his theology book *The Greatest Universal Sureties*, the translation of which will be published soon, Lord willing.

1) Intelligent Muslims, those who genuinely and sincerely care about their faith, will pack and move to the Muslim world, i.e. Dār al-Islam, and if they're not able to they will move out of the mainstream, i.e. out of sight and out of mind, possibly even off the grid, far from large towns and cities.[204]

2) Those who stay in the mainstream, i.e. those who associate with or follow organisations like CAIR, ISNA, RIS, FOSIS, MCB etc., will end up "practicing" an Islam that will be unrecognisable to the overwhelming majority of Muslims living outside the Anglosphere. Their beliefs, laws and customs will no longer be regarded as Islam but will instead be seen as something completely separate, such as "American Islam" or British Islam". The advocates of these localised "Islams" will compromise and alter whatever they can in order to be tolerated by the majority, host population. The organisation Muslims for Progressive Values is a good indicator of where these people are headed.[205]

3) The rest will apostate, either formally or in practice, i.e. they might call themselves "secular Muslims", or "cultural

---

[204] There will also be less intelligent and less informed Muslims who will be *forced* to leave, either by law, e.g. they will not be granted citizenship or permanent residency, or by the circumstances, e.g. the majority populations will make it clear that Muslims are no longer welcome and these Muslims will finally realise and act accordingly.

[205] http://www.mpvusa.org/ (Accessed Dec 29, 2016)

Muslims", in the same way that Richard Dawkins is a "cultural Christian".[206]

That is the future, but one does not have to be pessimistic. Praise Allah and thank Him that this religion has authorities that look after it and its people, and these authorities warned several years ago that this would happen. There is no need to be shocked or saddened. Rather, we should be grateful and at peace, because the Lord is in control of His affair, and we should prepare ourselves. Allah's earth is vast. Turn to Him and you will always find somewhere to worship Him in peace.

---

[206] https://infogalactic.com/info/Cultural_Christian (Accessed Dec 29, 2016)

ABOUT THE AUTHOR

Mahdi Lock is a teacher, student, blogger, podcaster, writer, and professional freelance translator of classical Arabic Islamic texts into English. He has been studying theology, law and other Islamic sciences for several years with teachers in England, North Africa and the Middle East. To date, his translated works include *Kitāb al-Ḥalāl wa al-Ḥarām* by Imam Abū Ḥāmid al-Ghazālī, *Kitāb al-Waqf* from *al-Mughnī al-Muḥtāj* by al-Khaṭīb al-Shirbīnī, the introduction to al-*Majmūʿ* by Imam Yaḥyā al-Nawawī and *Sharḥ al-Ṣudūr* by Imam Jalāl al-Dīn al-Suyūṭī.

Printed in Great Britain
by Amazon

40172879R00093